UNCLE MONDAY
AND OTHER
FLORIDA TALES

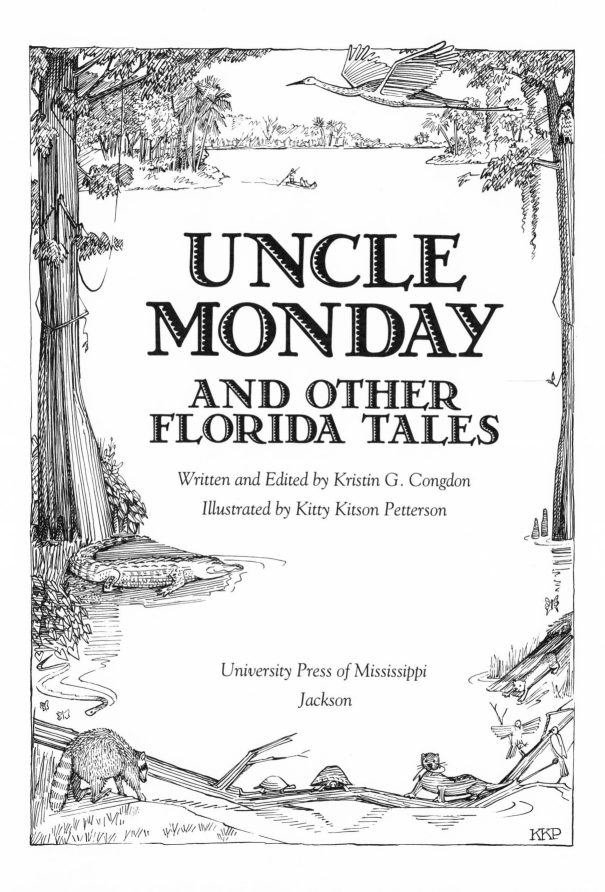

UNCLE MONDAY
AND OTHER FLORIDA TALES

Written and Edited by Kristin G. Congdon

Illustrated by Kitty Kitson Petterson

University Press of Mississippi

Jackson

www.upress.state.ms.us

Designed by John A. Langston

∞

Library of Congress Cataloging-in-Publication Data

Uncle Monday and other Florida tales / written and edited by Kristin G. Congdon ;
illustrated by Kitty Kitson Petterson.

   p. cm.

  Includes bibliographical references.

  ISBN 1-57806-384-1 (cloth : alk. paper) — ISBN 1-57806-385-X (pbk. : alk. paper)

   1. Tales—Florida. I. Congdon, Kristin G.

GR110.F5 U53 2001

398.2'09759—dc21   2001022620

British Library Cataloging-in-Publication Data available

This one is for "Mabel the Whale."

—*Kristin G. Congdon*

To Rick, my husband and beloved companion.
Through the good times, and the scary ones.

—*Kitty Kitson Petterson*

CONTENTS

AUTHOR/EDITOR'S PREFACE

In the spring of 1969, along with three college friends, I drove from Valparaiso, Indiana, to Pompano Beach, Florida, for spring break. A friend's parents, who lived in Michigan, had a condominium in Pompano Beach and were willing to let their daughter entertain three ready-to-party and ready-to-sun-worship chums. We drove all night, figuring we could sleep on the beach when we got there. There are many tales that have been told about that trip, but working on this book reminded me of one that I haven't told since I came to Florida in 1988. It "feels" better telling it out-of-state. Nonetheless, I relay the story here, claiming the stupidity of youth as my excuse.

My roommate Lori and I were both dating fraternity guys from Valparaiso University at the time, and, for both of us, the relationships were fairly serious. In fact, we both married these boyfriends and have stayed married to them all this time. I can't say if it has anything to do with the gift we brought them back from Florida during that spring break trip or not, but I doubt it.

While we were soaking up the sun, cruising the streets of Fort Lauderdale, and enjoying a week of irresponsible living apart from our partners, we wanted very much to purchase gifts for our boyfriends back home. When we saw that you could have a baby alligator shipped anywhere in the United States for a few bucks, we decided that was it! We purchased them without a second thought, and when we returned we told everyone that a great surprise was coming soon in the mail. It took months, but the little creatures did arrive.

Lori's boyfriend, Steve, an ecologically minded outdoorsman from Minnesota, was furious. Dumb move on our part, he claimed. I don't remember what happened to his alligator, but it survived for a while. I don't remember it living as long as David's did.

David put his alligator in a box and kept it well fed for a number of months. Of course it grew. There came a time when he had to go home to Fort Wayne, Indiana, and, lacking a volunteer alligator-sitter, needed to take the reptile with him. This was not an easy task, since he drove a Volkswagen Beetle and needed to pack up numerous other belongings. As anyone might imagine, the alligator was not embraced when he brought it into the house. His parents were dog lovers, but in their retirement years had no animals, since they wanted the freedom to travel without restraints. My mother-in-law-to-be, Ruth, hated reptiles.

The alligator, which had grown considerably, was kept under David's bed on the second floor of the house. One day, when he came home, he discovered that the alligator was missing. It was later found dead in the swimming pool. Of course, I was upset, but David never seemed to mourn the loss much. ("What did you expect?" he often asked.) But I haven't held him responsible for the reptile's demise, which was most likely, I figure, owing to chlorine. Ruth was mum about the entire thing. Her only comment was, "Wonder how that alligator made it to the pool?"

Things have changed in Florida since the late 1960s, and I have changed as well. I would never consider taking an alligator out of its natural environment, unless it was a threat. It was a foolish thing I did back then. As a college professor, I hope my students have better sense, but then again, times are different, and you couldn't buy an alligator on a street corner to send to Indiana nowadays anyway.

That 1969 trip was my introduction to Florida. Back then, I never dreamed that I would end up in this amazing state, feeling more at home here than in any of the other eight states where I have lived. Since coming to Florida to live in 1988, I have enmeshed myself in the study of various Florida cultures. I have done fieldwork in the traditional ranching community of Christmas, the historical African American town of Eatonville, the Spiritualist community of Cassadaga, and the muck farms of Apopka. I have attended local Asian and Latin festivals and have visited many artists who are experts in such traditional expressions as Norwegian hardanger, surfboard making, sword swallowing, quilting, produce-stand construction, and Russian icon painting. I have found Florida to be far more than the theme parks and retirement homes many people, especially those from out of state, conjure up in their minds when they imagine its landscape. My work as a member of the Florida Folklife Council and the Florida Folklore Society, years attending and participating in the Florida Folk Festival, and work on several exhibitions and folklife projects have served to teach me about the ways of Florida living. Though I have lived in Florida a relatively short time, my feet feel rooted here.

The idea for this book came several years ago. Kitty Petterson and I were having lunch together, discussing her gallery and her decision to close it because of a drastic increase in rent. Kitty had already established herself as a well-known local artist who did paintings of humorous scenes of daily life, but she was looking for a change. She explained that she wanted to illustrate children's books. Knowing about the lack of books on Florida's traditional tales that could be accessed by children, I suggested she illustrate Florida's folktales. It sounded like a good idea to her, but she needed a collaborator. I decided I couldn't pass up the chance to work with her on this project. While I had a strong background in folklore and knew enough about Florida to take on this project, I was not an expert on traditional tales. After several years of reading, interviewing, and getting help from my friends, I feel I know a lot more.

This book is intended for use by children, youth, and adults. We hope that educators, librarians, scholars, and parents will find it to be a good resource. It is designed to be both educational and entertaining. It can also be used as a springboard toward the creation of new tales, a better understanding of old tales, and the retelling of tales the reader has previously heard. The illustrations are added for aesthetic pleasure, a fuller engagement with the tales' content, and as visual documents of one interpretation of what is in the mind's eye. This book has been a pleasure to compile. Kitty Petterson and I have been introduced to wonderful, inventive storytellers, both living and dead. These storytellers make up a good part of Florida's cultural fabric.

This book is a collaborative project, as is the telling of traditional tales. Many people deserve recognition and thanks. I begin by thanking Tina Bucuvalas, Florida's state folklorist, for reliable assistance with the selection and identification of the tales, help with background information, and an early reading of the manuscript. She has been a trusted expert. Teresa Hollingsworth, who, at the beginning of this project, worked with Tina in the Florida Folklife Program, Division of Historical Resources, Department of State, also reviewed the manuscript and offered encouragement. From her new position at the Southern Arts Federation in Atlanta, she has continued to offer support.

Many others helped and deserve thanks. Maria Redmon translated some of the tales from Spanish and offered help with contextual information. Brent Tozzer searched the State Archives for Seminole stories. Sandra Johnson, director of the Pensacola Historical Resource Center, gave permission for four traditional tales to be reprinted. Ann Hoog, at the Library of Congress, assisted with two stories from the archives. Without their assistance this volume would not have its breath of diversity. Other organizations gave permission to reprint stories: University Press of Mississippi, University of Florida Press, Libraries Unlimited/Teacher Ideas Press, *Journal of Southern Folklore*, the Will McLean Foundation, and the Florida Department of State, Florida Folklife Programs. I am grateful for their enthusiastic support and assistance.

My thanks goes to the University Press of Mississippi, especially to Craig Gill and Anne Stascavage for overseeing this project and to Tammy Oberhausen Rastoder for her careful editing.

Without the storytellers who shared with me some of their favorite stories, this book would not have been possible, or at least it would be terribly lacking in contemporary lore. This book is a tribute to your love for traditional stories. Many thanks to Myra Davis, Ada Forney, Chuck Larkin, Liliane Nerette Louis, Phyllis NeSmith, Richard Seaman, Jim Bob Tinsley, and Stephen Caldwell Wright.

I also acknowledge the writers from the Florida Writers' Project who documented so many of the traditional tales retold in this book. Our memories of the past are richer today because of them. I thank Stetson Kennedy, who worked with the Works Progress Administration heading up the Florida project, for his suggestions, encouragement, and all the work he has done throughout his life to preserve and make visible Florida's rich and diverse culture.

Many other individuals assisted with background information, reviews, and story suggestions. My gratitude goes to Erika Brady, Ken Buchanan, Alexandra Curran, Ormond Loomis, and Russell Reevers for their knowledge about Florida's culture, for their suggestions, and for being there when I needed help.

I am especially grateful to Stephen Goranson, who for Christmas two years in a row gave me hours of free editing and helped with some of the research. He kept me sane with the detail "stuff" that I don't often enjoy. Thanks, bro.

Thanks also to David Congdon, my husband of thirty-one years, for caring about Florida's folklore as much as I do. He has continued to support me during this time-consuming project, and I love him for it.

Kristin G. Congdon

ILLUSTRATOR'S PREFACE

From the early years of elementary school, every Saturday morning my sister Susan and I would walk to the Fulton, New York, Public Library and haul home dozens of books, all we could manage to carry. Then we two little girls would settle into worlds of astonishing facts and glowing fantasy, reading practically nonstop until the pile of books was read. Before long we had consumed all the books in the children's section. Then we were granted the unheard-of privilege of having our very own adult library cards when still barely tall enough to see over the checkout desk. I often wondered if the librarians or my parents exercised censorship. I don't recall experiencing any restrictions on what I read at all.

I do remember the vivid pictures and words that formed in my mind. I studied the illustrations, sometimes loving them, sometimes feeling that I could do a much better job! I had discovered that I could draw, too, and draw I did. I loved the feeling of crayons and pencils, the smell of newsprint and tempera paints, the feel of the apron I wore to protect my clothes. As I grew older, my art tools expanded to include the soft shading of graphite, the crispness of pen and black, black ink, the limitless colors and so many varieties of pigment. I always knew that creating art would play a vital role in my life.

But I had many other roles to fulfill too, especially wife to Rick, who led me all over the world, and mother to Kristine and David, who now both enjoy the thrill of creative careers. She is a writer of children's books and magazine articles; he creates beautiful city maps and web sites that combine art and function. They have all endured years of dealing with my sometimes scattered efforts to combine my art with family and civic functioning. I thank them profoundly for the love and support they have given me.

The stories in this book are a fascinating reflection of the truly unique state of Florida and its varied cultural influences. I thank the storytellers who preserved this part of our heritage. Without the words, the images couldn't exist.

To Kristin's thanks to those who assisted her in assembling this grand collection of folklore, I add mine. I feel privileged to be entrusted with the exacting job of creating visual representations of these traditional tales, and I thank Kristin for including me in this project.

I could not have accomplished my part without the help and understanding of those around me. I thank my husband Rick for being tolerant of spending so many weekends entertaining himself and managing household necessities. I thank my daughter, Kris, and her husband, Mike, for their input and interest, and my son, David, for his interest and encouragement. I thank those other family members, friends, and associates who are excited about this project and eagerly anticipate its publication. Their enthusiasm has kept us going. Both Kristin and I hope the result exceeds your expectations.

Kitty Kitson Petterson

INTRODUCTION

This book is designed to be used in a variety of ways by all age groups. I have edited the stories in such a way that children and teenagers, as well as adults, might enjoy reading them. The introductions before each tale provide contextual information for the story to be appreciated and understood historically. The "reflections" are offered to encourage creative dialogue about the traditional tales. Parents, teachers, and librarians may find these questions useful when reading to children. Some older children might find the reflections self-motivational. The first chapter of this volume describes traditional storytelling in Florida and, hopefully, will be of interest to those readers who want to spend more time learning about the practice of passing on tales in the southernmost continental state where almost anything seems possible and the stories about the people and events are as exciting as any told anywhere.

Most of the older tales in this book come from the Florida Writers' Project and were found in the Department of State, Division of Historical Resources, Florida Folklife Programs Archives in Tallahassee. The Florida Writers' Project was part of the Federal Writers' Project, which was a subsidiary of the Works Progress Administration (WPA). This was President Franklin D. Roosevelt's effort to get the country back on its feet during the Great Depression. The Federal Writers' Project began in 1935 and lost its federal funding in 1939. Its main contribution was the American Guide Series of more than four hundred books. Many states, like Florida, were able to keep their offices open on shoestring budgets until 1943 (Taylor 112; McDonogh vii–xxxv). Out-of-work writers were hired in the forty-eight states and U.S. territories to provide us with a multifaceted self-portrait. The result was a view of United States' residents from all walks of life at a time when the country was in terrible crisis from a suffering economy. From this effort came numerous publications from 1935 to 1939, including one hundred full-sized books (Taylor 103). Despite a great deal of early negative criticism, the result was eventually highly praised. Besides giving us invaluable documents about our history, the Federal Writers'

Project employed writers who desperately needed employment, many of whom thrived on the camaraderie and group purpose. At the height of the effort, the Federal Writers' Project had 6,700 employees and 12,000 volunteer readers and editors. Among the writers who received jobs were Richard Wright, Ralph Ellison, and Florida's Stetson Kennedy and Zora Neale Hurston. Famed poet W. H. Auden referred to the Federal Writers' Project as "one of the noblest and most absurd undertakings ever attempted by any state" (Taylor 106).

The Florida Writers' Project was ambitious. Numerous unemployed writers went off the dole, traveling all over the state to do interviews (Findlay and Bing 292). Information from these documents is now seen as invaluable to the study of history and folklife in the state. The state was recognized then, as it is today, as having a character unlike any other state in the union. Seekers of gold and seekers of sunshine have invaded it—people from all over the world. The Florida Writers' Project documents emphasize contrast and variety, confusions and consistencies, just as this book of traditional tales portrays (McDonogh ix). The diverse cultures are depicted with historical information, jokes, proverbs, cures, curses, legends, myths, tall tales, fables, family histories, and various other bits of folkloric information.

The project's research on Florida's Negro alone resulted in more than 2,500 pages of information, including 72 interviews with ex-slaves. None of these documents, however, were published until Gary W. McDonogh compiled them in 1993 (ix–x).

Stetson Kennedy, born in 1916, was a native of Florida who, at the age of twenty, began working as a junior writer interviewing Cubans in the Florida Keys. Reflecting on the experience, his first with Cuban culture, he said, "In spite of all the hardships [of the Depression], they were having a ball. They were really enjoying life in a way that I'd never seen anybody enjoying life. . . . I've never gotten over it" (qtd. in Bucuvalas, Bulger, and Kennedy 169–70). He produced the Key West section of *Florida: A Guide to the Southernmost State,* and then moved to Jacksonville's state office, where he headed the unit on folklore. It was his job to convert interview notes into finished chapters for the *Florida Guide.* After his work in the Florida Writers' Project, he continued to work to promote Florida's folklore. He wrote books, including *Palmetto Country,* and was a founding member of the Florida Folklore Society (Findlay and Bing 293).

At its height, the Florida Writers' Project employed two hundred writers, although today most of them are unknown to us. No lists of who did the writing survive.[1] In fact, anonymity was valued. This helped ensure stylistic uniformity where the values of the times emphasized the accomplishments of the society rather than the individual (Findlay and Bing 291). One writer, however, besides Kennedy, who is remembered as being associated with the Florida Writers' Project is Zora Neale Hurston, who grew up in Eatonville, the oldest African American incorporated municipality in the country. Her tale about Uncle Monday is used as the title for this volume.

I selected stories from the Florida Writers' Project in the state archives that were not as well known as some of the other tales that are more readily available in other publications, such as the stories about Brer Rabbit. I made an effort to select tales from different parts of the state, representing different ethnic groups. However, in a state as diverse as Florida, not all cultural groups have been represented. For this I apologize, but the impracticality of the task prevented me from fully realizing this goal.

The selected tales also come from various times in Florida history. Many of the tellers are contemporary and the tales are personal. I approached them individually, as they were valued tellers in their community. The storytellers were ready and willing to share their stories with others and enthusiastic about being included.

The illustrations in this book are one interpretation of how a scene from the story might look in the mind's eye. When a story is illustrated, it adds to the voice of the speaker, and it conveys something new to the meaning of the tale that the language doesn't readily provide. They are examples of how an artist's vision can enhance a tale. These illustrations are provided to increase the magic and the pleasure of the storytelling process. They add to the storyteller's voice.[2]

While scholars continue to debate the meaning of terms such as *fable, legend, myth,* and *folktale,* I have given definitions of these and other useful terms and relevant people in the glossary at the end of the book. These definitions are intended to guide the reader toward enjoyment of the tales, and not as hard and fast categorical definitions, which would take more of a complex discussion. A bibliography of useful books is also included. Information found in these sources aided me in writing the glossary and the introductory materials to the traditional tales.

Perhaps, at this very moment, some of the storytellers represented in this book can be found in their homes, at family gatherings, or at festivals repeating these same stories. Many other exceptional storytellers are probably telling legends, tall tales, myths, or fables in various locations around the state. Perhaps their children are learning the tales, revising them to better fit their time and space, so that they might pass them on to the following generation. It is my hope that the retelling of these traditional tales, and many others like them, does continue to occur throughout Florida. These stories provide us with a way to know and enjoy history and learn a little more about ourselves as we root ourselves more deeply in the swamps, cities, and beaches that have made Florida such an amazing state.

UNCLE MONDAY
AND OTHER
FLORIDA TALES

1

Telling Traditional Tales in Florida

Florida conjures up many rich, exotic, and amazing images in people's minds all over the world. It is southern, swampy, hot and sunny, and full of beaches, tourists, outlaws, alligators, mosquitoes, and a wide variety of ethnic groups. It is Cracker, Latin, African American, Afro-Caribbean, Asian, and Native American. It is a politically conservative state, yet many issues that are on the radical fringe have roots here. When we think about Florida, we think about music and the names Jimmy Buffet, Ray Charles, Eric Clapton, Gloria Estefan, K. C. and the Sunshine Band, Madonna, and Jim Morrison come to mind. Florida has Disney, citrus, sugar cane, the Space Coast and the Everglades, Bike Week, *Miami Vice*, spring break, bingo, theme parks, and Florida writers such as Dave Berry, Carl Hiaasen, Jack Kerouac, Tennessee Williams, and, of course, Ernest Hemingway. Our good weather attracts many sports figures. They include Chris Evert, Jack Nicklaus, Shaquille O'Neal, Arnold Palmer, and Pete Rose. The rich and famous come here to live, for at least part of the year. We know that Florida has been a home to the Kennedys, John Lennon and Yoko Ono, Burt Reynolds, Wesley Snipes, and John Travolta. With all these well-known names, news, gossip, and storytelling abound.[1]

Besides all that, Florida has been a setting for events that challenge our imagination, pique our curiosity, and cause us to want to pay attention with more intensity. Perhaps it is the quality of the light here that provides a kind of surreal quality to life. Colors are more intense, the sun is more spectacular, and the air can be sugar-sweet. It often does feel like paradise. But just when it seems like heaven on earth, a violent tropical storm appears with its ubiquitous and dangerous wind, water, and lightning. Indeed, those of us who live here worry about hurricanes, tornadoes, sinkholes, erosion, termites, droughts, floods, freezes, and overpopulation—all environmental threats. In Florida things easily grow and easily rot. You can get lost in its

3

urban areas and its swamps and junglelike terrain. We have muck that can suck you
down, sharks that can traumatically interrupt your leisurely swim, and get-rich
scams that read like science fiction. Florida has it all (except maybe snow and mountains). And its traditional tales are wild, rooted, and alive. Those of us who "own"
this state as our homeplace enjoy becoming involved in its history, its diversity, and
its traditional tales. We embrace the dialogue that traditional tales encourage, while
we are fearful of Florida's rapidly changing landscape as more wilderness becomes
pavement. Our traditional tales point out these changes to us as they teach us, entertain us, and help us determine our future identities.

Traditional tales are one aspect of folkloric study. Folklore has been said to be
"the boiled-down juice of human living" (Hurston, qtd. in McDonogh xx).[2] And in
this state, that "boiled-down juice" is in the air and in our landscape. Our landscape
may change with an influx of Haitians or Cubans, a new growth of retirees, Hurricane Andrew, or the recent wildfires that have scorched our forests. But changes in
our landscape may also have origins with changes that begin in our minds (Solnit
115). Someone sees the possibility for a new cruise line business, another theme
park, or yet another high-rise on the ocean. Florida changes, and we change. What
is clearer to us these days than ever before is our position as a part of nature. We participate in it, and our traditional tales are a gentle reminder of that fact. It has
become very difficult to think about the human species without also reflecting on
our interactions with nature and how we are able both to sustain and to threaten it.

Floridians have long been connected to the land. For example, the Panhandle,
as well as other parts of Florida, is known for its beekeeping practices (Burt 67),
which help sustain plant life, and everyone knows that Florida's early image as a paradise continues to compel tourists to visit in swarms. This image of the tropical
peninsula can be traced to the late Renaissance when the focus of thought was on
"an earthly rather than a heavenly paradise," thereby fueling a desire in the six-
teenth century for new world expeditions (Ammidown 240). Since the early European travels to Florida, others have encouraged images of Florida as a place to come
to. Stephen Foster, in 1851, for example, wrote the well-known song "Way Down
Upon the Swannee River," which was catchy enough to become popular and, in
1935, was adopted as Florida's state song.[3] Most old-time Floridians, however, are
aware of the fact that Foster probably never came to Florida and only used the
Suwannee River (which he changed to "Swannee") to fit the melody of his tune
(Burt 63).

Many of Florida's traditional tales, and our best storytellers, are well connected to the land. The Everglades is one area that is rich in folklore. Draining of the Everglades began in 1880, which not only drastically affected the wildlife, aesthetics, and ecological balance of the area but also changed the lives of people who lived there (Burt 229). For those who worked the land, known as "gladesmen," "the Everglades must be understood as more than a mere backdrop" to their cultural experiences (Simmons and Ogden xvii). They had to be expert observers of the landscape and their sense of identity was directly connected to it. Often spending weeks at a time in the wilderness, they would pole through the mazelike islands of mangrove trees in flat-bottom skiffs. Their livelihood, and that of their families, depended on catching game from the region (xvii–xx). Gladesman Glen Simmons described one such experience when he and a friend had gone into the Everglades to cut mahogany. "My partner at this point had had enough of the heat, rain, skeeters, deer flies, and pulling and pushing that loaded scow through mangrove trails, which were not large enough to accommodate a four-foot-wide-boat. It was as close to hell as a man wants to get—but at least I was used to it. I had never made an easy dollar anyway" (46).

In the Wiregrass region, which reaches into Florida's northwestern Panhandle, controlled burning is an important part of balancing the ecological system and allowing humans to live successfully on the land. Fire is important to many of the southeastern Native Americans who settled there before Whites. Billy Joe Jackson, a Creek Indian now living in Oklahoma, explained, "Fire is everything, there would be nothing without it. It is used to grow grass and to get rid of grass. To destroy things and to help one's self. There's got to be fire" (qtd. in McGregory xvii). In the Creek's worldview, people came from the sun, and to recognize and celebrate this origin from the power of the Supreme Being, fire always burns in Creek village squares (McGregory xvii).[4]

Because Florida's weather can be so harsh, times are often measured by the hurricanes and the droughts rather than by more human-made disasters like the depression. Glenn Simmons, for example, claimed that the roads were so muddy and bad during the 1940s that they had to hold road repair parties to get the fish trucks in and out (Simmons and Ogden 142). "The Big Freeze of 1894–95" destroyed Sanford's citrus industry, causing many growers to turn to celery as a cash crop. By the early 1920s Sanford was exporting $8 million worth of celery per year, so much so that it was called "Celery City" (Brotemarkle 75). While today droughts can be devastating in Florida, in earlier years, they were deadly. The spring of 1825 brought a drought so bad that many of the five thousand Seminoles living in Florida were left starving (Downs 41).

While catastrophic disasters perhaps are what Floridians fear most, the day-to-day aspects of the natural environment can be wearing. Simmons remarked that in Flamingo, the mosquitoes were often so bad that you could hear them roar. In order to ward them off, people had to build smokers from the black mangrove, which were kept burning outside the houses all summer long. He recalled: "Yea, people smelled like smoke. . . . Your old clothes would get kinda yellow looking. But, you know, nobody seemed to care" (Simmons and Ogden 129–30). On the other hand, the Everglades almost always provided food for the Simmons family. "We ate guavas and coco plums that grew along the glade edge. And she'd [Ma] make teas from the sweet bays in our yard. She'd also cook the wild pigeon peas that grew around the house. . . . And if a person was not in a hurry, enough food could be found around the gator holes, sloughs, and pinewoods to keep him alive" (19–20).

Florida's early settlers survived in numerous ways, as its landscape is so varied. Because its terrain was (and still is in places) so difficult to negotiate, fleeing Indians, runaway slaves, Civil War refugees, and others with adventurous souls came to Florida. The islands off of Key West were (and perhaps still are) used by drug smugglers (Burt 157), and violence of all kinds was not uncommon in this tropical territory. Many Wiregrass settlements were known as "tough towns," they say, because of excessive drinking (McGregory 71).[5]

According to Ste. Claire, Florida's frontier was as dangerous as any town in the West. In fact, what we know as cowboy life started here sooner and lasted longer.[6] Ste. Claire observed that if we want stories about tough cow towns, we need only look into the annals of Arcadia. "During the 1890s, Arcadia averaged 50 gun or fist fights per day. That action was all part of a thirty year war between cattlemen and rustlers along the ironically named Peace River" (16). A little farther north, Mulberry seems to have been no more peaceful. What was a sawmill town until 1890 soon became a phosphate center and a magnet for those seeking wealth. Along with the boom came saloons, dance halls, and fighting. "Every Monday morning there was a coroner's inquest to tote up official recognition of the weekend murders. From an old mulberry tree, at a spot where the railroads once dumped their freight, men were lynched. Against its trunk, some were shot. Law was often homemade and creative" (Burt 77–78).

Some Florida towns are steeped in tales of independence and feuding. Barberville, named for James D. Barber in 1882, is one such place. Barber's family had made a living from the land as ranchers as early as the 1830s. After the Civil War Barber refused to pay taxes, which caused great unrest with his neighbors and the law. David Mizell, the sheriff and a nearby rancher, responded by periodically taking a few cattle from Barber's herd. Barber threatened Mizell, and the sheriff was later murdered. Mizell's son sought revenge, killing members of the Barber family. This story, like many others of this sort, is ingrained in local lore (Brotemarkle 115). McGregory claimed that so many people were lynched in the Wiregrass region before the 1870s (more Whites than African Americans) that the result has been many ongoing tales about violence, mystery, and moral discomfort (72).

Perhaps owing in part to the challenges of living in such a complex landscape, religion has always been integral to the life and tales of Floridians. There are tales of the devil, of misfortune resulting from bad deeds, and numerous tales of how people came to be the way they are.

Just as religious preferences vary in Florida, so too do the kinds of people who populate the state. As Bucuvalas pointed out, "In comparison with many other regions of the United States, Florida is new and constantly changing. While some Floridians can trace a long family lineage here, most have arrived within the last 50 years. . . . Even Florida's Native Americans are [relatively] new" (4). Burt described Florida's population growth as follows:

> Throughout Florida history, wave after wave of newcomers invaded. One wave after the Civil War moved Florida's population from 140,000 in 1860 to 270,000 in 1880 (about 65 percent native-born). Other waves came along during the 1920s boom, jumping the population to 928,000 in 1920 and to 1.5 million by 1930, during the Depression. In a post–World War II surge, the leaps became even larger, more than tripling in the next three decades to some 9 million in the 1980s (about two-thirds born somewhere else). As the year 2000 approached, Floridians numbered some 14 million plus 40 million or so tourists each year. (12)

Florida's population becomes more diverse each year. Asians, Pacific Islanders, Native Americans, Haitians, Bahamians, Jamaicans, Cubans, Europeans, and African Americans are all part of the mix (Bucuvalas 4–5). A recent increase of

Hispanic (or Latin) immigration has now made Hispanics "Florida's largest minor-ity" (Padilla A-12).[7] There are approximately two thousand Seminoles and five hundred Miccosukee living in Florida today (Downs 3–5).

In the United States, cultural groups tend to prefer associating and living amongst those who share their interests. Whereas the suburbs used to be the place where Whites lived, today the suburbs are becoming the most common place for Hispanics to live as well as numerous other ethnic groups. This could well be the result of television, which sells the United States' suburban dream to people all over the world. So when immigrants arrive, this suburban dream is often what they have set in their minds (Edmondson 31–32).

Economically and environmentally this population increase translates differ-ently. The Southeast is "bursting at the seams," and quality of life is the most impor-tant issue. The Southwest's low unemployment is frightening businesses away while Tampa Bay, Central Florida, and Lakeland are more successfully attracting new busi-nesses. In the Northcentral area there is not enough new business, whereas the Northeast has so much growth that traffic and urban sprawl has become problematic (Economic Yearbook 56).

All these shifts in population and environment result in storytellers inventing new tales and remembering and re-creating old ones. People change occupations, and places take on new identities. DeLand, founded in 1876, was built on Harry A. DeLand's fortune from manufacturing baking soda in New York. In its early days, Mr. DeLand encouraged settlers to his new town by offering to buy back their land if they were not satisfied with the quality of life there (Brotemarkle 100). And when phosphate was discovered in Hawthorne in 1880, it became a place to go for work and prosperity (Burt 20). In the Panhandle and other parts of North and Central Florida, the turpentine business was what sustained many people. In the Wiregrass region, workers often received names that related to the kinds of jobs they did. They were called "stillers, deckhands, haulers, dippers, and chippers" (McGregory 32). The African Americans who worked these jobs often sang songs that are fondly remembered by the Whites who listened to them. One remembrance is that the rhythms chimed in "with the music of the wind in the treetops" (qtd. in McGregory 33).

Many folkloric beliefs have become integrated. Florida's early Indian popula-tions, for example, were quick to accept runaway slaves, and Black culture and Seminole life melded. Though the African Americans were often taken in as slaves, they lived more independently with the Seminoles than they had with Whites

(Downs 34). In the Everglades both Whites and Indians hunted alligators, and in the process grew more culturally compatible (Simmons and Ogden 66). Crackers of Celtic descent shared many customs and attitudes with the Indians. While much has been written about the conflicts between these two groups of people, it is important to recognize the ways in which they admired and understood each other. They were both traditionally organized in clans, both had close emotional ties to the land, and both believed that supernatural spirits inhabited the woods. They enjoyed dancing, sacred fires, and a history of being strong warriors (Downs 20). Likewise, Blacks and Seminoles often shared traditional tales. Hurston and others found very similar tales in the legends of Seminoles and African Americans, like the story of how the rattlesnake got his rattle (McDonogh 14). Intermarriage and familial relationships amongst Whites, Indians, and African Americans were not uncommon, making for cross-racial sharing of traditions.

Marjory Stoneman Douglas, in her 1967 book *Florida: The Long Frontier*, wrote about the shift in Florida's population after the Civil War: "They [Crackers] had taken the place of the almost vanished Indians in the remote country where they kept alive the legends, the ballads, the tunes, the customs of their Georgian, Carolinian, Scotch-Irish, Irish, English, or even German ancestry. They were, as they had been, proud, secretive, unlettered, suspicious, enduring as time" (qtd. in Ste. Claire 56). Cracker traditions became so important in the 1970s, when Jimmy Carter was elected to the presidency, that the term "Cracker Chic" was coined (Wilson and Ferris 1132).

Keeping traditions alive is important to all cultural groups. Traditional tales are often the strongest in groups where oppression has been a way of life. African Americans' expressive communication system helped foster self-pride while it "taught techniques of transformation, adaptation, and survival" (Hemenway xx). Hurston's way of explaining what happened at Eatonville's traditional storytelling place, Joe Clarke's store, was to relay an old Black folk song:

> Got one mind for white folks to see,
> Nother for what I know is me;
> He don't know, he don't know my mind.
> (qtd. in Hemenway xxi)

Racism and other oppositional forces often resulted in the creation of expressive metaphors. For example, Virgil Hawkins, explained the difference between racism in the North and the more visible form in the South in the 1930s and '40s: "It's just like walking on a carpet with a snake in it. I'd rather see the snake out here so I can hit him than to have him hiding in the carpet and I don't know when he's going to bite me" (qtd. in McGregory 90).

While African Americans have inhabited Florida for a long time, many Blacks continue to come from the Caribbean area hoping for a better place to raise a family. When immigrants from the Bahamas and Cuba came to South Florida and the Keys in the nineteenth century, they found the "color line" more stringent in their new homeland than it was in their old. Marked discrimination was imposed in the workplace, educational system, and day-to-day social system. In Key West, Blacks, regardless of where they came from, were confined into a "Colored Town" on the eastern end of the island, west of Whitehead Street (Bucuvalas, Bulger, and Kennedy 174).

Other new residents of Florida came in their later years for retirement. South Beach, for example, was a haven for retirees in the 1980s. Many of these older adults would sit on benches by the beach, feed pigeons, and tell stories to each other (Burt 195).

The content of these tales, of course, varied. But for many of Florida's old-timers, stories about local legendary people top the list of favorites. And this state is full of characters, those who could tell a great tale and those who were the focus of great tales. Perhaps our best known storytellers are Zora Neale Hurston and Marjorie Kinnan Rawlings. But there are many others, including Rawlings's husband, Norton Baskin, who loved a good Cracker tale (Burt 39–54).[8] John M. DeGrove told entertaining stories about feeding moonshine mash to the mules and cows (215), and Jimmy Jones was full of tales about the history of Florida's horse racing. He could tell a great tale about missed investments, creating new bloodlines, and "why benign climate and limestone in the soil made Marion County such good horse country" (182). Noah Cook, from Carrabelle, longed for the simplicity of the past. He claimed that the world was being taken over by "fast-talking parakeets lugging around boxes of paper" (12).

In 1976 Carl Allen was voted Florida's Number One Cracker by a survey taken by the Florida Bicentennial Commission. He was one of the great "keepers of the culture," and much of his tradition was rooted in the food he served in his restaurant in Auburndale, west of Lakeland. Allen not only told Florida tales, he was the center of many tales. Burt described his restaurant: "The walls and ceilings were lined with early Florida memorabilia—rifles, plows, Indian arrowheads, horse gear, lanterns. You sat at tables that once were sewing machines, drank iced tea from fruit jars and could order (in addition to rattlesnake) fried rabbit, armadillo, mullet, turtle, catfish and even ordinary chicken and cornbread" (19). About the rattlesnake, Allen explained that he had "some boys that hunt 'em for me. Bring 'em in alive." But he also killed them himself to ensure their freshness for his patrons (20).

Another great old-timer whom many Floridians remember with fondness was Ross Allen. A stuntman in the old Tarzan movies and an alligator man, he was a naturalist who mourned the loss of Florida's wilderness and the arrival of Mickey Mouse (150–54). Besides these notable individuals and the legendary heroes and heroines portrayed in this book, there is also Paul Dickman, who made Ruskin famous for his tomatoes (73), and the many pirates who frequently attacked United States ships before Florida became a state (Brotemarkle 151).

Many of Florida's tales, as one can readily see from this volume's table of contents, include animals. Bloodhounds, imported from Cuba as early as 1837, were often used to track escaped slaves and unwanted Indians. Tales abound of how the hunted were able to avoid capture by these animals (McDonogh 25). Panther stories are also ubiquitous, as Crackers love to tell about their interactions with this now-rare animal (Burt 16).

Alligator tales are always popular in Florida. Kevin McCarthy recently wrote an entire book on *Alligator Tales*, which, no doubt, only includes a small number of the alligator tales told around the state. He pointed out that when visitors come to Florida, they routinely ask to see alligators (1). In response to this request, some alligator trainers have taught them to do tricks like going down a slide into a pool or holding open their mouths while a brave soul places his (or sometimes her) hand inside and the audience gasps in delight (15–17). There are also a number of farms and zoos available for tourists to visit, like Gatorland in Orlando. Ross Allen worked at the Silver Springs attraction for forty-six years interacting with alligators, leaving there in 1975. In 1981 he came up with an act that was meant to produce genuine anxiety in his audience. He planned to open another tourist attraction, called Alligator Town, U.S.A., which would feature his youngest son, Sidney, who would dive into a pond of twenty alligators, stay down long enough to make people nervous, and then come to the surface holding a small alligator for his father. Allen died before the venture became a reality, but his legend as the "alligators' Buffalo Bill" lives on (Burt 150–51).

Alligators are so ubiquitous here that they can become architecture (as in Gatorland, where you enter through the gator's mouth), claw back scratchers, and, of course, the mascot for the University of Florida (McCarthy 40). Wrestling alligators has been a tourist attraction for many years, and some Seminoles and Miccosukees made a living from such performances.[9]

One 1910 tale in McCarthy's book is about an alligator that was used to clean the sewers in Tarpon Springs. Apparently the man in charge of keeping the city's drains clean found this a convenient way to do his job. "He first put a large brush at the end of a long rope. At the other end of the rope, he attached a chain which he put around an alligator's neck. As the alligator makes its way through the sewer, his swishing movements enabled the brush to clean up the debris" (165).

Another tale, told by Glenn Simmons, explains how he hid alligator hides from the authorities. After all, selling hides was the way he made a living. He revamped a Model A into a truck with a box in the truck bed that few knew about. One night he was pulled over with about one hundred hides tucked away from sight. These alligators represented several weeks of work, and Simmons didn't want to lose them. He proudly reported that they were not detected. That box saved him many times (Simmons and Ogden 120–21). Simmons recounted that gator tales and other experiences in the Everglades were often told to friends and relatives at the end of the day, often around campfires and smoking smudge pots. Sometimes they sipped moonshine while rehashing these adventures and other tall tales (xix).

Fishing tales are also very popular, owing to Florida's numerous beaches, lakes, and rivers. Fishing enthusiasts come to fish Florida's waterways from all over. Lake Okeechobee is a favorite spot. Burt reported that some of the catfish caught there weigh as much as the boys who bait the lines—"sixty pounds and more according to tales" (139). Reportedly, there was one catfisherman who lived in the Lake Okeechobee area and liked having his shoes shined on Saturday nights. They say it puffed up his ego. But he disliked wearing shoes, and he often lost them when he got into fistfights with local rivals. As a result, he started getting his bare feet shined (Burt 145).

Sometimes the fish stories are more like pranks. Glenn Simmons recorded one such tale:

Back about 1924, my oldest brother, Emmett, brought home a sambo mud fish [or bowfin, Amia calva]. Down on this end of the glades mud fish used to be plentiful. They are big old, black, ugly things. Now you don't hear much about them, and that's good. Well, they die slow out of water. My middle brother, Alvin, said, "Put your finger in his mouth, Glen." And the damn fool me did. Then the mud fish closed his mouth on my finger. Well, Pa heard me hollering and come a-running. He took a knife and pried the fish's mouth open. Then he said to Alvin, "Now put your finger in his mouth." Large saw palmettos and pine grew close to the house, and they soon covered my brother's escape. He didn't take time to say good-bye. He gave the mud fish time to die before returning home. (Simmons and Ogden 13)

Sometimes the folklore revolving around the fishing industry has to do with selling fish instead of catching them. One Jacksonville fish peddler in the 1930s named Jeremiah would chant this work song:

Je'miah got fresh fish,
Je'miah got fresh fish,
He got mullets, he got shrimps,
He got brims, he got trouts,
All Je'miah wants you to do is come out.
(qtd. in McDonogh 48–49)

Tales can also be told about eating fish. One of the state's oldest festivals, the Florida Seafood Festival, is held at Apalachicola. They have an annual oyster-eating contest, with six competing contestants. Tales about winners and losers can often be heard there (Burt 186).

Many other Florida stories revolve around the cattle industry, which has held its importance in the state since it began in the 1500s (Ste. Claire 173). Because ropes and lariats were fairly useless in Florida's thick scrub, trained dogs were used to round up cattle. Called "catchdogs," these canine helpers were as important as the bullwhips that were sometimes popped to communicate messages to others on the opposite side of the range (175). Stories were often told in cow camps where cowherders would meet at the end of the day. With Florida's junglelike terrain, a distinctive culture was created, with place-bound traditions and tales (51). Many of these traditional tales are told repeatedly at festivals around the state. Cowman culture, for instance, is celebrated annually at the Silver Spurs Rodeo and the Kissimmee Bluegrass Festival in Central Florida (Brotemarkle 81).

There are so many festivals in Florida—more than five hundred a year—that one might say the state is "festival crazy" (Burt 184). The history of festivals in Florida goes way back. Both African Americans and Whites in Pensacola, for example, in the early part of the twentieth century, celebrated Mardi Gras with an elected King and Queen and a night ball (segregated by race). A parade was held where elaborately decorated floats represented legends, fairy tales, and "mythical personages" (McDonogh 61). Both Blacks and Whites participated in the Gasparilla Festival in Gainesville, an event that celebrated José Gasparilla, a pirate who made routine trips to Port Tampa. African Americans enjoyed participating because it was believed that he took Black sailors and runaway slaves with him on his voyages. Floats representing these boats populated with Blacks were made to highlight that aspect of his legend. In the 1930s, schools in Eatonville would close for the South Florida Fair, which took place in Tampa. Games were played and contests were won most often by students from Eatonville's Hungerford Academy (60).

Other events, while perhaps less formally choreographed, display a festival atmosphere. Daytona Beach's Bike Week is one such popular gathering. During the first week of March, the beach attracts all kinds of bikers, from those who ride full time to businesspeople, teachers, and others who enjoy the leather clothing and the roar of the Harley-Davidsons (Brotemarkle 123). Tales of biking adventures go along with admiring tattoos and cruising on bikes.

Tourists come to Florida for a variety of other reasons. Orlando is the number one tourist designation in the world because of the theme parks—most notably, of course, Disney World. Built on forty-nine square miles of land acquired in 1965, it transformed Central Florida from a quiet little town to a sprawling city filled with malls, hotels, traffic, souvenir shops, and service jobs (9–10).

Tales about Disney are so common that they are now part of the cultural landscape of Orlando. Although I have never seen them, I understand that Disney has an entire underground environment where workers "hide" parts of the operation that they don't want visitors to see, including trash and costume changes. Students of mine who have had jobs as Disney characters claim that one of the things you have to be most careful about is that there are not two Mickeys or Minnies in the park at the same time.

Urban legends about Disney are so popular that a web site has a special category for them. One tale about Walt Disney is that he was an illegitimate child of a Spanish woman from Mojacar, in Andalucia, Southern Spain. She was engaged to a young man from her village who tragically died in Morocco before they wed. As the story goes, she was left pregnant and gave the baby up for adoption to a couple from the United States. Only just before she died did she hear that the child she gave up had become the famous Walt Disney. This tale is said to be false, but it has the making of a good fairy tale and is repeated often.

Many other stories about Walt Disney continue to be told. His face is reportedly superimposed on the theme park's Haunted Mansion and his body put in cryonic storage. Tales about Disney films include one about Donald Duck being banned in Finland because he wears no pants. Speculation about *The Lion King* is whether a swirling cloud of dust spelled out the letters S-E-X as Simba, Pumbaa, and Timon look up at the stars (Urban Legends, Sept. 9, 2000, *http://www.snope.com*).

A few years ago, Florida's tourist market was damaged by a series of tourist murders, which, coupled with a number of environmental disasters, created a kind of paradise lost. This became a matter of utmost concern for a state where image is perhaps more important than reality (Lippard 134). The way people feel about Florida and the stories they tell about it directly determine how the tourist industry will fare at any given time.

But long before Disney built its empire in the central part of the state, tourists were coming to seek other kinds of experiences. Glenn Simmons recalled that as he got older, the Everglades changed because of weekend hunters who used airboats, small airplanes, and glade buggies to catch their prey, pushing traditional "glade-skiffers" to the sidelines (Simmons and Ogden xxii). The automobile and the interstate systems were even more influential in transforming Florida, making it easier for tourists to come and go with relative ease (Ammidown 239). Appealing promotional articles about Florida became commonplace in magazines such as *Scribner's Monthly*, *Harper's*, and *Frank Leslie's Illustrated* (241). In the late 1930s and into the 1940s the American Guide Series was publishing brochures and books, thereby increasing the appeal of tourism and adventurous travel (Findlay and Bing 290).

Small roadside attractions of every imaginable kind were created. They were frequently based on the environment—"the springs, the forests, the wildlife—and they were often intertwined with a narrative extrapolated from Florida history" (Ammidown 239). White Springs had one of the most popular spas. Reportedly, the Seminoles used to bring sick braves to the White Sulphur Springs to "take the water," since it was said that they could cure almost any physical or mental illness (Burt 64–65). Perhaps because of the associated belief that the Fountain of Youth could be found in Florida (Ammidown 246), this was the place where all kinds of people believed they could come to be healed.

Before motels were commonplace, local governments established locally run tourist camps, and an association of "The Tin-Can Tourists of the World" was formed. Annual camp meetings were held along U.S. Route 27, otherwise known as the Orange Blossom Trail. It ran from Ohio through the central part of Florida. The main camping sites for tourists could be found along this road. The Tin-Can Tourist association had their Christmas meeting and homecoming in the town of Arcadia (Ammidown 243). One can easily imagine how campers shared travel experiences with each other, citing the best restaurants, parks, and attractions to visit.

Among the earliest roadside attractions, developed in the 1920s and '30s, were the roadside gardens. Ammidown points out that even the name "Florida" represents a feast of flowers, which conjures up images of a garden paradise (241). These gardens included McKee Jungle Garden, Monkey Jungle Gardens, and Parrot Jungle. These garden spots welcomed visitors looking for pleasant experiences rather than threatening ones provided by viewing other kinds of creatures such as alligators. At Cypress Gardens, founded in 1936, one can still enjoy beautiful flowers, water skiing acts, and young women dressed in antebellum costumes with huge hoopskirts (Ammidown 252).[10] According to Ammidown, "The small attractions can be separated into thematic categories: Florida as a magical source, or shrine (the springs); Florida as Eden (the garden attractions); Florida as the underworld (the alligator and reptile attractions)" (243).

Residents and tourists alike take an interest in launches at the Space Coast. Some people claim that the night watches are the best, especially the first three seconds. They say it is like daylight for a few moments (Brotemarkle 159). Every time a spacecraft is scheduled to go off, thousands of people line the highways and step outside their homes and workplaces to watch (Brotemarkle 157). It is as if the entire area is collectively and miraculously fixed on the same thing. Stories about failed space ventures and why they happened abound. They are often connected to UFOs, life on other planets, and mysterious disappearances. The Space Coast's existence in Florida's eastern seaboard also provokes tales about government secrets and cover-ups. I have heard people who work at the Space Coast whisper their experiences quietly, for fear of reprisal.

These kinds of "hush-hush" tales, told with warnings that someone might get arrested or fired from their jobs for telling what they know or feel to be true, are common. For instance, tales about drug smuggling and moonshine are commonplace. Glenn Simmons reminisced, "During those days in the 1920s and '30s, you had to be closemouthed about moonshiners and everything else. Anyway, what they did was their business and none of mine. Although I came across many of those men in my travels, I knew to keep my mouth shut. If I'd been married, I wouldn't have told my wife about them" (Simmons and Ogden 48). After time passes, however, it becomes safer to tell these stories. One tale is told by John DeGrove, whose family roots are in Palm Valley: "One guy had a still out back of his place. For security he kept a bunch of guineas. They're good watchdogs. They make a lot of noise when someone comes around. He also had nine daughters" (qtd. in Burt 218). His daughters would climb trees and act as lookouts.

Florida, like the rest of the United States, is full of exceptional storytellers. Charles Kuralt, reflecting on his travels around the country, explained it like this: "Hardly a week goes by that I don't come across a poet at some country crossroads. I don't mean a writer of verse. I mean somebody who has inside of him [or her] such a love of something—farming, flying, furniture-making—and talks about it, [in such a way that] he [or she] makes you love it too" (Kuralt 89). The experiences and knowledge these individuals have is often expressed in the form of a story. Kuralt, however, enjoyed not only the content of the narrative but also its process and its form. He went on to say, "If you take the time to listen, you can hear much unrhymed poetry in the air of America—in the singsong chant of the auctioneers, the jargon of the truckers on the CB radio, the bawdy jokes of construction workers, the lazy gossip of neighbors, [and] the extravagant tale-telling of tipsy strangers in a bar" (89).

Many scholars and everyday people recognize the importance of storytelling. Jerry Mander reasoned that when a story is told, the audience has the opportunity to become just as creative in the listening role as the teller is in the telling role. Pictures are created in your head that can go far beyond the mere words. In this way, the teller can be seen as a stimulus for the imagination of others (112). Storytelling teaches us history, ecology, and folklore (McGregory xix). It becomes part of the cultural landscape, and, when a traditional tale is told, the work of cultural preservation is being done. Artistic practices that connect with audiences, that make relationships stronger, as opposed to fracturing them, build on the development of community life (Gablik 157–58). Often a teller will relay a story as if it belongs to him or her, even if it is not a personal experience. If told well, it has a sense of authority to it, and the narrator has a command of the text as it is presented. Various dramatic devices are selected and used, and the audience enthusiastically receives it (McNeil 12). Every time a traditional tale is told, it communicates something about our past.

Historian David Lowenthal asserted that we should be more aware of our histories but that a fixed past is not what we need. Instead, what we need is "a heritage with which we continually interact, one which fuses past with present" (410). Lowenthal states that we go looking into the past in literature as a way of "explaining the past, searching for a golden age, enjoying the exotic, reaping the rewards of temporal displacement and foreknowledge, and refashioning life by changing the past" (22). All these reasons for engaging in our past and enjoying traditional tales have relevance. He recognized that, to a great extent, our past is how we create it. Certainly this can be said about the past we create from traditional tales. What is most important today is how we think about our past in terms of our present and future. Lowenthal asks that we use today's insights to understand the meaning of the past. In this way, he said, "we may breathe new life into it" (410). Perhaps this is one reason that traditional tales have such an appeal for us. We continue to tell them, rethink them, change their content to make them more relevant, and bring the present into an understanding of how we are and how we must act because of the stories that make up our multiple histories.

Folklorist David Whisnant reminds us that while there is much to admire in southern culture, our cultural traditions are also full of hateful actions, like violence, racism, sexism, and classism. He noted that we must recognize these aspects of our culture and work to change them in the present by engaging in acts of critical thinking (7). For this reason, I have added the "Reflections" after each tale. They are intended to help us think about our identities, our heritage, and our place in cultural practices. In Chinese, the word for "tradition" also means "good manners" (Kingston 171). It is my hope that the practice of reflection, whether done individually or in groups, as you read through these tales, can be done with good manners. It is through this kind of practice that new ways of interacting and understanding our past and the traditions of others can be explored.

Lowenthal observed that each "inheritance demands to be both revered and rejected. . . . Any effort to balance the past's benefits and burdens implies some awareness that we need to cherish the past and also to get rid of it; either course of action embodies inherent contradictions" (74). The telling and retelling of tales, therefore, must be about both stability and change. "We cannot function without familiar environments and links with a recognizable past, but we are paralyzed unless we transform or replace inherited relics" (29). We would be well served to recognize the violence that is our heritage as Floridians, citizens of the United States, and our more global society. We should strive to become different, more peaceful people because of it. We ought to learn to cherish the Florida that we still have, with its swamps, beaches, forests, mullets, fortune telling, grapefruits, coconuts, catfish, alligators and crocodiles, Spanish Moss, cool waters, and the smell of jasmine and orange blossoms in the air. We would benefit from recognizing and celebrating our many and varied residents who have tales of immigration, often terrifying and, thankfully, sometimes accommodating. We need to remember our histories that are full of tales rooted in war and violence, hatred and fear, so that we may learn to build our lives and futures on a different and better kind of experience. We need to rejoice in the fact that Florida is still a paradise where dreams can still be dreamt, the odd can still be enjoyed, and experiences replete with humor, adventure, and pure pleasure may still be found. Traditional tales remind us of all of this.

How Things Came to Be
the Way They Are

Every culture has stories, or myths, about how the world began, and how things came to be the way they are. Myths, in this book, are stories that show us ways of understanding the unknown. They express matters of utmost importance while tales and fables often address other concerns. Myths relay a sacred history, often an event that took place at the beginning of time. In reading or hearing myths, one encounters something real, learning about the beginnings of an animal, an island, a behavior, or a species of a plant. These kinds of stories are about creation, and the characters are usually supernatural beings. They are known for their actions at the beginning of time (Eliade 5–12). While not all the traditional tales in this section are myths, many of them are.

Today many people use the term *myth* to mean a lie. *Webster's College Dictionary,* for example, while acknowledging a traditional meaning of myth that explains cultural practices, also defines it as "a belief or set of beliefs, often unproven or false, that have accrued around a person, phenomenon, or institution." Paula Gunn Allen claims that this use of the word discredits the beliefs and worldviews of those of us who do not belong to a dominating group. In other words, we think our myths are truth, while the myths of others are falsehoods (102).[1] It is important for us not only to connect (and reconnect) with our own myths but to encounter and move into the mythic space of others. In this manner we can explore the world and its possibilities in a broad range of ways. As we learn about our neighbors and about individuals around the world, we discover new ways of seeing and open up creative venues for thinking about the meaning of life.

Some say that having myths in our lives today is crucial. Carl Jung felt quite strongly about the importance of myths and claimed that they may be even more sustaining in our lives than economic stability (Gablik 52). Paula Gunn Allen describes the importance of myth this way:

> Myth functions as an affirmation of self that transcends the temporal. It guides our attention toward a view of ourselves, a possibility that we might not otherwise encounter. It shows us our own ability to accept and allow the eternal to be part of our selves. It allows us to imagine a marriage between our conscious and unconscious, fusing the twin dimensions of mind and society into a coherent, meaningful whole. It allows us to adventure in distant, unfamiliar landscapes while remaining close to home. Thus myth shows us that it is possible to relate ourselves to the grand and mysterious universe that surrounds and informs our being; it makes us aware of other orders of reality and experience and in that awareness makes the universe our home. (116–17)

Knowing myths can give us power. For example, the Cuna Indians believe that a hunter who knows the origin of his game will be more successful with the hunt. And if animals are to be domesticated, this can more easily be accomplished if the secret of their creation is known. In a like manner, you can safely hold a poisonous snake or a red-hot iron, if you know about the origins of the snake or the fire (Eliade 15).

Perhaps the best known scholar of myths is Claude Lévi-Strauss, whose extensive work is called *Mythologiques*, available in English as *Introduction to a Science of Mythology*. In it, he analyzes more than eight hundred American Indian myths taken from different times and cultures dispersed over two continents. His thesis is that there is a seamless chain of mythological being and a single logic to mythmaking. He posited that concepts that populate myths such as sound, light, hunger, and silence are conceptual tools for understanding more abstract ideas with which we all struggle (Gardner 33–34). Bruno Bettelheim claimed that myths and fairy tales give us security within our worlds by giving us answers and solutions to problems (51), and Irving Howe pointed out how important it is to us to have explanations for how the world is constructed other than those provided by linear logic. If science is our only answer, we engage in the world without a moral orientation. The world becomes a mechanical place and our orientation in it is less meaningful (Gablik 46). Indeed, many stories in this section can be used to nourish moral insights.[2]

Some of these origin stories (also called "foundation myths") have been handed down from one generation to another, often for many decades or even centuries. Others are relatively new, created to answer current questions. Some are combined with tall tales, making them humorous and more unbelievable. But all these traditional tales are intended to delight the audience while they provoke the imagination.

"Why Men and Women Don't Have Tails Like Cows" is an African American parallel of the Adam and Eve story with which most of us are very familiar. "How the Gopher Turtle was Made" also makes reference to the creation story in the Bible. It makes sense that it would focus on gopher turtles because they were ubiquitous in the early days of Florida's settlement. Glen Simmons, who grew up in the Everglades in the early part of the twentieth century, claims that before the 1935 Labor Day Hurricane there were hundreds of gopher turtles on Cape Sable. He relays his personal narrative about how he and a friend tried to make money off of capturing masses of gopher turtles only to find that they weren't very valued as a food source (Simmons and Ogden 134).

Animals are often central to origin stories, in part possibly because they used to be more overtly prevalent in our lives, especially in Florida before the advent of grocery supermarkets, modern housing, and air-conditioning, which keep us inside during the warmer parts of the year. But Floridians still love to tell tales about animals. For example, on a recent visit to Key West, I heard that the island was full of eight-toed cats, all descendants of Ernest Hemingway's pets.[3]

This section also contains the Seminole tales, "Why the Rabbit Is Wild Today" and "Stolen Fire." Much of the Seminoles' folklore and history remains in oral form only today, although more information about them is now being recorded (Downs 10). Their religion, along with that of the Miccosukees, is based on the teachings of Breathmaker, who gave them Florida. This supernatural character taught them how to live on this "pointed land" with the birds and animals that inhabit the space with them. This is evident in that Rabbit is able to talk to the Seminoles in their folklore. It is interesting to note in "Stolen Fire" that Rabbit visits during the Green Corn Dance, which is still the Seminoles' most important ritual. It features a sacred fire, medicine bundles, new patchwork to wear, games, and dancing. When this ritual takes place, healing, unification, and new beginnings are possible. Storytelling, during this event, is always central (Downs 7, 259–60). Tradition in Native American cultures is important because at its core is nature, and nature must not be transgressed in order for people to survive. While some Anglo views of tradition might be, in some respects, seen as a separate entity that can be measured, for the Native American, tradition is everything, permeating like time (Coe 46–48). Therefore, the telling of origin stories by Native Americans (and this is also true for many cultures) is about what directly concerns them (Eliade 11).

While the tales in this section are about how the world began and how it ought to work, they are more than that. They are about coherence and integration; they are poetry and art; and they assist us in being emotionally related to the experience of being human. As Paula Gunn Allen explained, these tales provide "a holistic image to pervade and shape consciousness, thus providing a coherent and empowering matrix for action and relationship" (105). While Gunn and others suggest a lofty goal for origin tales, these tales can be approached on many different levels. At the very least, they may simply be enjoyed.

WHY MEN AND WOMEN DON'T HAVE TAILS LIKE COWS

This tale was told by an African American storyteller named Uncle Ike to a White man who came to visit a lake near Tallahassee in the early 1900s. It is one of many Adam and Eve stories that are told throughout Florida. The story is more humorous than the Genesis version since it incorporates a second theme about our relationship to an animal—in this case, the cow.

This story is a myth because it is based on an event that took place a long time ago as one way of explaining the origins of things. The story is basically religious prose that is handed down from generation to generation.

A LONG TIME AGO—long before the wars—the good Lord made the world. And then He rested for a day. The next morning, He decided to plant a garden in the world. When He finished it, He called it the Garden of Eden. It was a beautiful, colorful garden with all kind of flowers and trees. Fruits and berries grew on the trees and vines. He was pleased with what He had made.

Then one day He thought to Himself that a garden needed somebody to live in it. So He made Adam, the first man. Adam was kind of lonesome, so the good Lord took pity on him and made him a wife. Her name was Eve, and she was the first woman. Adam and Eve were just like men and women today, only they had great long tails like cows. The tails were occasionally useful in that they could swat a troublesome fly or create a bit of a breeze when it was hot.

After Adam and Eve had seen the garden, God spoke to Adam. "Adam, this garden is for you and Eve. Stay here and take care of it. Use anything in it, and you may enjoy any of these fruits and berries." But then God pointed to another tree and said, "But you see this tree with the yellow fruit on it? Don't you touch that tree. It's mine." Adam replied, "Yes Lord, I understand."

Not so long after having that conversation, God left the garden early one evening. Adam knew He was gone 'cause he heard the garden gate go "click." About that time, Adam was walking around, enjoying the flowers and shade trees, when he looked up and saw the forbidden tree with the yellow fruit! It was the one the Lord told him not to touch.

Adam looked at it, and looked at it, and looked at it. The yellow fruit looked so lovely. He thought it must taste sweet and delicious. But Adam remembered God's words. This was God's fruit, and Adam was not to eat it. Although he tried to resist, Adam couldn't stop thinking about what that yellow fruit must taste like. At that moment, God's yellow fruit looked so much better than all the fruit on all the other trees. No other fruit seemed quite as special.

Adam became so tempted, he finally plucked one of the yellow fruits from God's tree. No longer able to resist, he stuffed it into his mouth. It tasted so delicious that he plucked another, then another and still another. Adam kept on eating and eating. After a few hours he had stuffed every piece of fruit on that tree in his mouth until there was no fruit left.

When Adam went to sleep that night, his belly was very full. He was so tired from eating all that fruit that he slept really hard. Adam kept on sleeping until late into the next day.

It was then that the Lord came back to the garden. Being God, He knew what Adam had done, and it made Him really mad. God was so angry that Adam would have eaten His fruit that He didn't even take the time to open the garden gate. He just put His hand on the wall and leaped over it. Then He went straight to the forbidden fruit tree.

When He got there and saw the tree, He was madder than ever. Last night the tree had been full of ripe, beautiful fruit. This morning there was hardly a scrap of fruit to be seen. Every piece had been eaten. He looked again, and He saw that the dirt around the tree had been trampled down. He looked this way, and He looked that way. But He didn't see Adam or Eve. Adam had woken up just minutes before and decided he better not be around that tree when God returned to the garden.

The Lord called "Adam." No answer. "Adam."

Adam hid behind a big oak tree and said nothing.

Then God called again, "Adam, you come here now!"

Adam figured he couldn't hide from God forever. God was too powerful. So Adam came inching up to God, because he knew God knew what he had done. Adam was very afraid of what his punishment might be.

When Adam finally got to within a few feet from God, the Lord asked, "Adam, why did you eat the fruits from my tree?"

Adam looked at the ground, not wanting to own up to his bad deed. He scraped his foot in the dust and said, "It wasn't me. It was Eve."

God shook his head, further disappointed in Adam. He knew better than that. God told Adam, "That story won't work. Just look at the great big footprints around my tree. Eve's feet aren't that large."

Then Adam got scared, and he ran for the bushes. God quickly ran after him.

But Adam had trouble running. He couldn't go very fast because his long cow tail dragged way behind him in the dust. Adam had eaten so much he didn't have the strength to lift it from the ground. He tummy was still so full of the yellow fruit that he had to run with lots of extra weight. Still, he was very fearful of how God might punish him, so he ran and ran. Try as he did, he couldn't outrun God.

It didn't take too long for God to catch up with Adam, at least close enough to grab his tail. He grabbed it in His two hands, set His two heels into the ground, and pulled. The tail came right out of Adam's behind by the roots. Eve watched in amazement.

And that's why people today don't have tails like cows do.

REFLECTIONS: *What would happen if Adam had a different kind of animal tail rather than a cow's tail? Would the story be the same or different? Can you tell the story from Eve's point of view? What was she thinking and doing while Adam was eating the fruit? What about Eve's tail? In your mind, what does the forbidden fruit stand for?*

HOW THE GOPHER TURTLE WAS MADE

This African American myth explains why we have two kinds of turtles in Florida. One lives in the water; the other is the gopher turtle, which lives on land. This story is not only about the origin of things, but about naming and the importance of communication. In many cultures, creation is directly connected to speaking. In this story, naming the turtle has a great deal to do with defining what it is and where it lives.

The gopher turtle is often referred to as a gopher tortoise. For some early white settlers, the gopher tortoise was a delicacy they called "scrub chicken." It is now illegal to kill and cook them.

ONE DAY GOD was sitting down by the ocean making fish. He made a whale, threw it into the water, and it swam off. He made a shark and threw it into the water, and it swam off. He then made mullet and shad-fish and trout, and they all swam off.

While God was busy making His fish, the Devil was standing behind Him looking over His shoulder. The Devil quietly watched for a while.

After making lots of fish, God made a turtle and threw it into the water. It swam off. About then, the Devil said, "I can make one of those things." The Devil thought a turtle would be fairly easy to make.

God replied to the Devil, "No, I don't believe you can." God knew that He was the creator of the world, and not the Devil.

The Devil insisted, "I can so make one of those things. Ain't nothing to making them anyhow. Who couldn't do that? I can't blow the breath of life into it, but I sure can make a turtle."

The Devil seemed so sure of himself that it made God a bit irritated. So God decided to challenge the Devil. He said, "Devil, I know you can't make a turtle, but if you think you can, go ahead and make one, and I'll blow the breath of life into it for you."

You see, God was sitting down by the sea making fish out of sea-mud. But the Devil went on up to the hill so God wouldn't see him making his turtle. So the Devil's turtle was made out of highland dirt.

God waited nearly all day before the Devil came back with his turtle made out of highland dirt.

As soon as God saw it, He said, "Devil, that isn't a turtle you've made."

The Devil flew into a rage. "This isn't a turtle? Who says it isn't a turtle? It sure is a turtle!"

God shook his head and said, "It sure isn't a turtle, but I'll blow the breath of life into it like I promised."

The Devil handed God the thing he called a turtle, and God blew the breath of life into what the Devil had made. Then God threw the highland dirt creature into the water. It came out. God threw him into the water again. He came out again. God threw him into the water a third time, and he came out a third time.

So God said to the Devil, "I told you that wasn't a turtle." God knew that any real turtle would head for the sea.

Still the Devil persisted. "Yes, sir, that is a turtle."

By this time God was chuckling a bit. He said, "Devil, don't you know that all turtles love the water? Don't you see what you made won't stay in the water?"

The Devil was stubborn, and he wasn't listening carefully to what God was saying. After all, the Devil mostly wanted to win the argument. He insisted again, "I keep telling you, I don't care if it doesn't go in the water. That's a turtle."

The debate continued for hours. Finally the Devil became very tired. He realized that God was not going to give in and accept his highland dirt creature as a turtle. The Devil also knew he had to move on to other things. So, reluctantly, the Devil said, "Well, anyhow, it will *go for* one."

And that's why we have gophers today!

REFLECTIONS: *What is the difference between a turtle and a gopher? What do people from the Midwest mean when they talk about gophers? Is this different from the Florida gopher? How? If the Devil had made his creature from sea-mud, do you think he might have been able to create a real turtle? Explain your answer.*

HOW FLORIDA GOT THAT WAY

Stetson Kennedy, one of Florida's earliest collectors of stories, recorded this tale. He first heard it in the 1930s from Carl Dann, who lived in Orlando. This origin story explains why Florida's landscape has some hilly areas. Not only is this story a tale about why Florida is the way it is, it is a also a tall tale. These humorous, exaggerated stories are often associated with the forming of the American frontier. The teller generally relays these stories as if they were the honest truth. The subject matter, as in this case, usually has to do with male-dominated occupations and daily activities.

MY GRANDFATHER came to Florida in a covered wagon in the 1860s. Being born in Pennsylvania, he was disappointed to find Florida so flat. So he got down on his hands and knees and scraped up the sand and dirt and built all the hills you can see scattered over Florida. He was so busy creating hills that sometimes he scared me with all his digging.

Sometimes he dug so much dirt out of the ground that he left huge holes in the landscape. Once I said to him, "Grandpa, you better not dig up *all* that sand and dirt. You have already created lots of places down here in Florida where you now have to use a ladder to climb up to the ocean." That's how deep he sometimes dug to get the dirt for his hills.

But he wouldn't pay any attention to me. Grandpa just went right on with his hill building. There was no doubt about it. My grandpa wanted to make sure there were hills in this flat land.

One time when he was digging, a wild buffalo charged down on us. I immediately ran and hid behind a tree. It looked like a mighty fierce buffalo, but Grandpa stood his ground. When that buffalo got within half a foot from my Grandpa, he stopped and opened his mouth real wide. Grandpa just ran his hand down that buffalo's throat, grabbed him by the tail, and turned him inside out! That threw the buffalo in reverse and made him go charging off where he came from. You see, my grandpa was not only determined to build his hills, he was brave as well.

While my Grandpa was born in Pennsylvania, he was mostly raised in Wisconsin, which presented other problems. You see, while Grandpa loved the hills of Pennsylvania, he remembered the lakes from his boyhood in Wisconsin. And he missed those Wisconsin lakes just about as much as he missed his Pennsylvania hills. So he hitched up his ox team and went over to the East Coast where he dipped up water with gourds and carried it back and filled up all the holes he had dug. That's the way he made all our lakes and rivers. He even gave them crazy names like Withlacoochee, Hickpochee, and Econlockhatchee.

And that's why we have hills, lakes, and rivers with funny names in Florida today.

REFLECTIONS: *How much of this story do you think is true? Does it matter? Do you have a grandparent who tells you stories about how things got to be how they are?*

CAPE SABLE CATS

This is a family tale told by Buster Roberts from Homestead in 1940. It is about how his father, Gene Roberts, saved Cape Sable from the rats.

CAPE SABLE is a peninsula off the southern tip of Florida. It is swampy and hot and one can only imagine what it must have been like in the early twentieth century with a rat problem.

In 1908 the manufacturing of syrup was the chief industry of Cape Sable, a peninsula on the southwest tip of Florida. People who lived in Cape Sable depended on their backyard gardens to supply them with food. But the sugar cane that was used to make the syrup and the gardens were both being destroyed by hoards of rats. These pesky animals had invaded the fields and the houses. Many acres of cane were completely destroyed after almost reaching maturity. The syrup mill was idle. The situation was very critical, and most of the Cape Sable residents were ready to give up and leave the peninsula.

The few cats on Cape Sable were fat and healthy and didn't seem to care about catching the pesky rats. However, one day, much by chance, my Pa, Gene Roberts, was sitting on his porch when he saw one of his kittens mauling a rat. Something seemed to click in his brain. "Cats!" he said. "That's the solution to our problem."

That night he called a meeting of the Cape Sable residents at his house. "Friends," he said, "we've done everything we know to do to get rid of the rats, and nothing has worked. I don't plan to spend any more of the few dollars I have left to buy poison. We've spread it all over the fields and houses time after time. But these darn rats won't eat poison. Why should they when they can eat our crops?" Pa's guests listened intently, agreeing with their host.

After a moment, he said, "Now I have a plan, but don't laugh at it until you think it over." My Pa took in a deep breath and continued, "How about us chipping in and going to Key West and buying a bunch of cats?"

Loud whoops of laughter greeted this suggestion, and Pa began to think he would be the laughing stock of Cape Sable. Gradually, however, they quieted down and thought a little more soberly about his plan. This, at least, was a straw to snatch.

Most of the people in that room had all of their worldly possessions tied up on the Cape in one way or another, and they hated to admit defeat.

Finally one of the men said, "Gene, I've never heard of such a thing in my life, but I'm willing to try it if the rest of the boys are." After some discussion, it was decided that they would use their remaining money to buy cats.

A few days later Pa set sail for Key West. As soon as he tied up there, he posted a sign that had been prepared before he left Cape Sable. "Will pay ten cents apiece for every cat delivered to this dock." Soon there was a steady stream of children bringing cats to sell. Every one brought was promptly purchased. When Pa had bought four hundred cats and spent forty of the fifty dollars he had brought with him, he realized that there was no more room on the boat for any more cats. They were all over the boat! "That ninety mile trip was the worst I ever made from Key West to the Cape," Gene declared. "Them darn animals squirmed and howled and meowed all the way home."

When Pa got home and let that bunch of cats out of the boat, they say it was the worst mess anyone had ever seen on the Cape. They went helter-skelter in every direction. They didn't know which way to go or what to do. The old-timers who were there got a kick out of talking about it. And some people talk about it still today.

We saw those cats around there for two or three years. Some folks say they went wild and bred with the wild cats, but not many people believe that story. Maybe bad weather and mosquitoes killed them all. But one thing's for sure. They've never been bothered with rats on Cape Sable since then.

REFLECTIONS: *Can you describe what it would be like to take a boat ride with all of those cats? What would happen when they were all set free? Can you describe the experience from a rat's perspective? How else might the people of Cape Sable have solved the rat problem?*

THE ALLIGATOR AND THE EAGLE

The Seminoles tell many stories about alligators, which is one of their favorite animals. This makes sense, because after the Seminole war of 1855–58, this group of Native Americans settled in the swamp and sawgrass region we call the Everglades. Here, in the mid-nineteenth century, they hunted, fished, and gathered food. Alligators lived all around this area as they do today.

This fable is another 1930s story from the Works Progress Administration. In those days nearly every Indian hut had an alligator pen near it. In this story the Seminoles tell about the loud "Ah-ah-ah!" the alligator makes when he is surprised.

WHEN THE WORLD first began, as we have been told, nothing but birds and animals lived on the earth. All of them could talk.

One day the birds set a date to play ball. The birds, large and small, gathered on the arranged day. One large, strong bird threw the ball higher than anyone else had. An old alligator was lying in the sun watching the birds play. He was angry because he was not invited to play with them. When he saw the ball go high into the air, he made magic and kept it in midair. All the birds flew about trying to bring the ball back to earth, but it could not come down.

After a long time, the alligator let the ball drop and caught it in his mouth. The birds tried in vain to pry his mouth open. A wise and cunning eagle sat on a rock and watched the weak, helpless little birds fluttering around the great reptile, begging him to return their ball. Finally he decided to help. He flew down and pinched the alligator's back with his sharp claws. The alligator was so surprised that his mouth flew wide open and he hissed "Ah-ah-ah!" at the eagle. As he hissed, the ball dropped out of his mouth, the birds quickly seized it and flew away. That is the reason the alligator opens his mouth and hisses "Ah-ah-ah!" to this day when he is surprised.

REFLECTIONS: *Have you ever heard an alligator say "Ah-ah-ah?" How would you react to hearing this sound from an alligator? Make up a story and tell us about someone hearing an alligator for the first time.*

BUZZARD ROOST

This is one of the humorous folktales that explains how a certain place got its name. Stories like this one not only draw attention to a specific site, but also focus on animals or birds that live in the area.

ACCORDING to the "Legend of Buzzard Roost," there has always been a feud between the owl and the buzzard. About fifteen miles from Pensacola, along the Escambia River, is a high rock wall. Here, one night a buzzard came to roost. That same night an owl, thinking he would get ahead of the buzzard, brought another owl to roost with him. But the buzzard had the same idea, so that night there were two owls and two buzzards roosting on the high rock wall. Each night the number of owls and buzzards grew until, finally, the buzzards outnumbered the owls since there are more buzzards than owls in this part of the country. The owls gave up their roost with the excuse that they would not continue to roost near such an inferior class of buzzards. The buzzards continue to occupy the roost and the place has become known as "Buzzard Roost."

REFLECTIONS: *Identify a place in your neighborhood that needs a name and create a story to go with the name. Tell your friends the story and see if it sticks.*

WHY THE RABBIT IS WILD TODAY

This Indian folktale is about the rabbit, who is the trickster animal for the Seminoles and the Miccosukees. Coyote usually plays this role for the Southwest Native Americans, and the raven is the trickster for Northwest Native Americans. This is a tale that researcher Frances Densmore heard from Josie Billie, who was a respected medicine man in the early part of the twentieth century. It is both an origin myth and a tale about the rabbit.

Native Americans tell many stories about animals, partly because their religious traditions place an emphasis on the kinship between humans and animals. Many tribes, including the Seminole, talk about a time when there was little, if any, distinction between them.

AT FIRST THE INDIANS were under the ground, in a big hole. Then they all came out to walk upon the earth. When they came out, they bathed in a little creek. When they got through bathing, they found they had nothing to eat and no fire to cook on.

One man, who held some knowledge, told them how to make the fire. He said to take dry, soft bark and twirl a stick between their hands. A spark would then light the bark. The first man got some dry punk, which is decaying wood. One man made the spark while another caught it on the punk. They made a great fire, but they had no food to cook.

Another man then heard a noise a half a mile or so toward the north. He thought some animals might be there. So he sent two men to get some little trees, and out of the wood from these trees, he made bows and arrows. When they were ready, he sent the boys and men to find something to eat.

They found deer, turkey, and bear and brought them back to camp. They now had plenty of meat they could cook over the fire. But they had nothing else to eat. They looked for something else and found swamp cabbage. A man cut it down and told the people to eat it raw, because they had no pots or kettles. As time went on, they learned to roast the swamp cabbage in the ashes of a fire.

They talked about how they were learning from each other, how one man knew

how to make fire, and another how to make bows and arrows. Still others could hunt, and some could cook.

Then one man said to another, "What shall we live in?" They had been sleeping in the grass but wanted more protection from the sun and rain. So they made themselves a house, like those the Seminoles live in now.

Then a horse and dog talked to one of the men. They talked like people. At that time the rabbit stayed with people, and he told lies all the time, but the dog and horse told the truth.

One day somebody found out that the rabbit lied. At that time he was always trying to be something he wasn't. He would go away, and when he came back he would say he had seen things that he had not seen. He would say he had seen snakes, alligators, turkeys, and turtles. The people did not know if they should believe this rabbit.

So one of the men said to the rabbit, "If you find a snake, kill him and bring him back to camp. If you find an alligator, kill him and bring him back to camp as well."

The rabbit then left the camp and found a snake. He killed it and started to bring it back to show to the people.

When the rabbit was bringing back the snake he saw an alligator. The alligator talked too, at that time. So the rabbit said to the alligator, knowing that the alligator could be a pretty dangerous character, "Somebody wants to see you back at the camp."

The alligator believed this and went along with the rabbit. When they had gone about half way, the rabbit tried to kill the alligator. Rabbit beat at the alligator but could not kill him. Pretty soon the alligator got tired of the battle, and he went back to his cave.

Then the rabbit came home with the snake.

When the man who had challenged the rabbit saw him, he was impressed. Rabbit had brought a snake, but not an alligator. But at that moment, the man thought he would like a turkey instead. So he said, "If you see a turkey, kill him and bring him home." So the rabbit started out to get a turkey, but figured it would be better to ask someone else to do the job. So he went to a wildcat and said, "You kill a turkey for me." Wildcat went and found a turkey and killed him. Rabbit brought the turkey back to the camp and told the man that he had killed it. The man believed the rabbit's story, and the rabbit continued to live with the people and tell his stories.

One day the rabbit wanted to get married. The man thought that because the rabbit had killed the turkey, he could provide for a family, so he married a girl. But, after the rabbit got married, he didn't bring any food at all. The people found out that the rabbit did not kill the turkey, so they drove the rabbit away from the camp. And that is why the rabbit is wild today.

REFLECTIONS: *What does this story teach you about lying? What does it teach about learning to make things? Can you continue the story? What might have happened to the rabbit when he left the camp?*

STOLEN FIRE

This 1930s Seminole tale was recorded by the Works Progress Administration. Fire, for the Seminoles, is one of the most sacred of all things. This story tells us how they came to possess fire. It refers to their sacred corn dance, which is an important ritual for many Native American groups, especially the Seminoles. In this ceremony they give thanks for the harvest, along with prayers for good weather for future crops. It often takes four days and includes a tribal council meeting, the lighting of the medicine fire, and ongoing dancing and storytelling. This ritual promotes social cohesiveness and spiritual rejuvenation.

Notice that the Seminoles, like many other Native Americans, use the number four, instead of three, in their storytelling. For them, four is a powerful number.

MANY, MANY MOONS ago there was only one Indian tribe that knew the secret of fire. The other Indian tribes tried ceaselessly to learn the secret. Each year when the Green Corn Dance was held, the Indians danced around a circle of fire. Indians from other tribes were always there, but could never get close enough to the fire to secure the secret. It was guarded that well.

One time the biggest, finest, most handsome rabbit the Indians had ever seen came to the Green Corn Dance, and begged to be allowed to dance around the fire with them. He could sing sweeter, dance better, and whoop louder than any person or animal they had ever seen. But the older Indians were suspicious of the rabbit.

They thought he might be a disguised Indian from a rival tribe, trying to steal the secret of fire. The younger Indians were more susceptible to his charm so the rabbit was allowed to take part in the dance. He danced closer and closer to the blaze, extending first one paw and then the other toward the fire. Suddenly he reached forward, grabbed a burning stick and, before the startled Indians could prevent him, disappeared swiftly into the forest.

After holding a council meeting, the wise people of the tribe decided to bring rain in order to extinguish the fire stolen by the rabbit. The medicine men went to the spring, and, for four mornings, made magic by charming the snake, who kept guard there. Torrents of rain came down, soaking the rabbit who was fleeing through the forest. The fire went out.

However, the rabbit did not despair, but attended the Green Corn Dance the following year. This time it was harder to persuade the reluctant Indians to let him dance with them, but they finally consented. Again he seized a burning stick and escaped to the forest. The medicine men made magic the second time, causing heavy rains, and the fire was again extinguished. For three consecutive years the rabbit succeeded in getting the fire, but each time the medicine men caused the fire to be put out by rain.

The fourth year the rabbit was wiser. After much persuasion, the Indians again allowed him to attend the Green Corn Dance. He obtained the fire and escaped. Again the Indians made the rains, but this time the rabbit hid under a coral reef and protected the fire under the shelter of the rock. When the rain ceased, he hurried to his tribe with the fire, and now all the Indians know the secret of fire.

REFLECTIONS: *What do you think the rabbit said to the Indians to allow him to come back to the Green Corn Dance after he had stolen from them? Why was it so important for all the Indian tribes to have the secret of fire? What would life today be like without it? Was the rabbit wrong to steal the fire?*

THE LEGEND OF THE MOSS

Florida is full of Spanish moss, vegetation that hangs on many trees and thrives in the humid climate. This tale explains how it came to be so plentiful. This story is repeatedly told throughout Florida.

Origin stories often explain certain aspects of nature. In doing so, plants, animals, and environmental forces such as the wind, take on human attributes such as speaking or having family ties.

"HOW DID THE MOSS come to the trees?" asked O-sowa one night as they sat around the campfire. She had been gathering moss that day, and wondered if anyone could tell her what animal had brought to her country the beautiful moss that made such soft, sleepy beds. "I will tell you how it came," said the chief. This is his story.

In Kan-yuk-sa, the land of golden sunshine and blue waters, the South Wind

was queen. She had ruled over the country for many moons and suns, and under her gentle sway the land grew more beautiful and fruitful as the years passed. Her subjects loved her as never a queen was loved before.

Now, the children of South Wind, the Little Winds, were also very dear to the inhabitants of this happy land. Like their mother, they brought joy and gladness wherever they went. When South Wind and her children traveled through the country the wild things of the forest were not afraid. They would come from their hiding places to meet them. Sometimes the Little Winds and the squirrels would play hide-and-seek among the great live oak trees. When the rabbits came from their hiding places, the Little Winds would tickle their noses and make them laugh and sneeze. Then there would be a grand race. Sometimes a rabbit would win the race and sometimes a Little Wind.

When the moon shone at night, and the rabbits came out to dance in the moonlight, the Little Winds danced with them. After their dances and games, the rabbits, the squirrels, and the Little Winds would go to sleep. But the Little Winds did not sleep very long; they were restless little people and liked to keep moving. So, often, while their playmates, the rabbits and squirrels, slept, they would fly up among the

treetops. While the mother bird stretched her tired wings and flew just a little way to get food and water, the warm, soft Little Winds would cuddle down in the nest with the eggs and keep them warm until the mother came back. Other Little Winds would rock the tree cradles, and when the baby birds came, all the Little Winds flew into the pine trees and sang them to sleep with beautiful slumber songs.

Mother South Wind was also very busy. She taught the corn to bend and bow when it looked toward its great king, the Sun, and how to grow strong and tall when the Moon Queen came to look down upon the earth.

Now, the North Wind hated the South Wind and her children. From the windows of his icy wigwam he watched day after day the beautiful country where everyone was so happy. When he saw the South Wind and her children dancing over the sunny land, he grew angrier and angrier. Sometimes he would mount a great snow cloud and fly down toward the land of flowers. But he never could get in, for the West Wind and the East Wind always drove him back.

Every year, during the moon of oranges, there would be a terrible battle between the East, North, and West Winds. The North Wind, though strong, was always defeated and went back to his icy kingdom wild with rage.

At last he appealed to the ruler of the world. "Oh, Great Spirit," he said, "is it fair that I should be driven away from the land of sunny Kan-yuk-sa, when all the other winds are free to roam at will over her forest and plains?"

The Great Spirit said, "It is not fair, North Wind. You, too, must be free to visit all parts of my kingdom, if only for a short time. You may go to Kan-yuk-sa, but you must go alone. Take no snow clouds with you and build no icy wigwams, for your stay must be short. The forests grow stronger for your coming, but the flowers sleep as if the everlasting silence had fallen on them and the birds fly far away!"

"It shall be as you command," said the North Wind, and he hastened back to his icy kingdom to prepare for his journey to Kan-yuk-sa. It did not take him very long to gather his forces, and soon North Wind and his white army were rushing toward the land of sunshine.

South Wind heard North Wind coming. She felt his icy breath and knew that alone she could never drive him away. So she called to her friends, East and West Winds, for help, and they called to their great friend, Mother Ocean. "Come to our aid," they said. "South Wind and her children are in danger."

"Do not fear, my fairies will help you," said the Ocean. "See, they come." As she

spoke, tiny mist fairies sprang from the sea and drifted toward the land. "Fly to the trees," they called to the South Wind and Little Winds. "Fly to the trees. We will hide you from the North Wind."

Away flew South Wind and her children into the trees, while all about and around the forests crept the mist fairies. More and more came in from the sea, until the land from shore to shore was wrapped in a soft gray mist cloud. The moon could not see through it, and neither could the sun.

North Wind and his army came, but they could not fly, for the mist fairies clung to their wings and made them heavy. They were soon lost in the dense gray cloud that hid the land, and they could not find a way out, though they tried day after day.

North Wind did not find South Wind, or her children either. So when the time came for him to go, he was very glad to leave.

When he had really gone, Mother Ocean called her children home. Then the sun called South Wind and Little Winds from their hiding places among the trees.

"Do not be afraid of North Wind when he comes again," called the mist fairies to South Wind and her children. "We have left many hiding places for you in all the trees. When you hear him coming, fly to them and you will be safe."

They were there, sure enough. All over the trees hung long, beautiful streamers of soft gray moss, just the color of the robes the mist fairies wore. The hiding places are still in the trees, and as long as they hang there the cruel North Wind will never be able to catch the South Wind and her children.

REFLECTIONS: *In what ways does this tale characterize the South Wind and the Little Winds as human? In what ways do people act like the winds? Do you have Spanish moss in the trees around where you live? In what kinds of trees can you find it? Do you know why it lives in some kinds of trees and not in others?*

3

People with Special Powers

Sometimes the main characters in traditional tales have unusual and legendary powers. Often they have massive strength or magical powers. Usually there is an element of truth or history in the tale. It is up to the reader or hearer of the tales to figure out which parts are based in fact and which aspects of the story are exaggerated or made up. Often these stories, and their heroes and heroines, are told to teach us a moral.

We are all aware of many of our country's most notable folk heroes. Johnny Appleseed was a friend to all as he sowed seeds to replenish the earth.[1] Davy Crockett was a Tennessee bear hunter, Mike Fink was a Mississippi keel boatman, Sam Patch was a cotton-spinner from Rhode Island, and Mose the Bowery was a New York City firefighter. According to folklorist Richard Dorson, all these folk heroes existed. But their legendary status grew in an extraordinary fashion (202).

Similar characteristics are often portrayed in tales about these heroes. For example, there is a group of folk outlaws (Jesse James, Billy the Kid, and Sam Bass) who share narratives with violent scenes and humor. They typically befriend the poor and are killed by a Judas-like character (Dorson 236). Values rooted deeply into the United States' culture can be explored in tales about these characters. Paul Bunyan, according to Dorson, represents "only the most obvious facts of American life—the worship of bigness and power, and the ballyhoo of salesmanship and promotion" (226). Boasting about physical strength, brawn, and muscle could be an expression of the discomfort that came with the machine age and the prospects of many people losing their jobs and identities.

While most of these stories focus on male characters, Florida is not without its female heroines. Yet when women are glorified in legendary ways, physical strength is generally not the characteristic that gives them prominence. For example, Mary

McLeod Bethune was the daughter of freed slaves. The fifteenth of seventeen children in her family, she gained international recognition for founding an all-girls
school in Daytona Beach in 1904. It later merged with the Cookman Institute for
boys in Jacksonville to form Bethune-Cookman College (Brotemarkle 127). The
tale that is told about her around Florida is that she started her school with a dream
and one dollar. She is honored and remembered as a role model for others who have
good ideas but few, if any, monetary resources.

Many of the tales in this section glorify heroes who know a lot about Florida's
natural environment. Because Florida's landscape can be so rugged and difficult to
manage, it makes sense that we tell tales about people who know how to deal with it
and cope in amazing ways.

Bone Mizell is one of Florida's most talked about legendary figures. He is enjoyed
because so many old-time Crackers like to celebrate Florida's ranching history,
which goes back into the early history of the United States. Ponce de Leon arrived
in Florida in 1513 and returned eight years later to settle a colony. The Caloosa
Indians forced him to leave, abandoning his herd of Andalusian cattle. These cows
are thought to be the first cattle brought to North America. Others were brought in
1539 by Hernando de Soto. Some of these animals were domesticated by the Indians while others roamed free. When the White settlers came and more successfully
established themselves in this tropical territory, a cattle industry was born. In fact, it
was Florida cattle herders who provided the Confederate Army with most of their
food. Today, Florida's cattle industry is alive and well, and Florida claims to be the
largest beef-producing state east of the Mississippi. In 1990 Florida had 21,000
working ranches, producing almost two million head of cattle (Bucuvalas, Bulger,
and Kennedy 39–40). Cowman events abound around Central and Southern
Florida. The Silver Spurs Rodeo in Kissimmee, which began in 1940, is so popular
that the Osceola public school system cancels classes for the day so children can
attend with their parents (Brotemarkle 82–83).

Bone Mizell is perhaps the most famous Cracker cowman. He was painted by
well-known artist Frederic Remington, who helped immortalize him. Though Remington remarked that Bone was "unkempt," he sought him out in 1895 as a model of
the southernmost state's cowboy image.[2] Local folklore claims that after Remington
encouraged Mizell to pose for him, mounted on his horse with his dog by his side, he
paid him off with a drink. Historian of Cracker culture, Dana Ste. Claire, claimed
that Bone Mizell was the "Crown Prince of All Cowmen." However, he was never a
king, because, like many folk heroes, he didn't want that kind of power on an ongo-

ing basis. Bone was a cowman's cowman. He was, after all, too much of a free spirit to be a king of any kind. He was a hard-drinking, fun-loving man who was said to be able to "'outrope, outride, outshoot, and outdrink' any cowman in Florida." Like many of the folk heroes from other states, Bone Mizell was also known for his generosity. He never had money for long, for he often shared it with friends. In fact he sometimes had so little regard for money that he was known to kindle his pipe with dollar bills. Born in 1863, Mizell died in 1921 in Fort Ogden, Florida (Ste. Claire 181–83).[3]

Besides tales about Bone Mizell, this section includes a story about Ole Man Davis, who was able to tame rattlesnakes. Along with the alligator, snakes are ubiquitous in Florida. Snakes have been associated with many things, including sexual drive, the underworld, the feminine, creativity, and the foundation of all life and energy (Lippard 35). We are repelled by them, we fear them, and yet we are, in some odd ways, attracted to them. According to folklorist Jerrilyn McGregory, snakes appear in many cautionary tales. E. W. Carwell, a resident of Florida's Wiregrass region, says: "Maybe we've instinctively feared snakes, since our distant ancestors feared and distrusted them for centuries. Remember the role the serpent played in the Garden of Eden? They were once worshipped as gods or friends of the gods, and they have been symbols of wealth, knowledge or wisdom in some parts of the ancient world. In ancient Greece, they were associated with the God of Medicine" (qtd. in McGregory 78). In Florida, snakes were often so plentiful and feared that some way of handling them needed to be devised.[4] Rattlesnake roundups took place in various parts of the Wiregrass region, and probably in other parts of Florida as well. In some places, especially in Georgia, these events were called rodeos. Awards are given to those contestants who catch the most eastern diamondback rattlesnakes or the heaviest snakes. Many people in this area and around Florida believe that when controlled burning was outlawed, nature got out of balance. One result of that was the proliferation of snakes (McGregory 109).[5]

Catching snakes may have been a less organized affair in other parts of the state, but some individuals were well known for this talent. Glen Simmons, from the Everglades, wrote about Mike Tsalickis, a Greek teenager he knew in the 1930s and '40s. Tsalickis was in the "live snake business" and had a roadside stand for tourists. He also took his snakes to a Greek-run tannery in Tarpon Springs. Simmons reported that Tsalickis taught him how to catch snakes: "To catch a nonpoisonous snake, he would grab it by the tale, swing it between his legs, close his leg, and the head would be trapped behind him whipping about. He then would slide one hand down the snake and then catch the snake's head when he got to the end." Simmons explained that this was done with lightening speed and that Tsalickis could catch a large number of snakes from a glade skiff at night with the help of a headlight. "It is clear that Ole Man Davis had ample opportunity to learn how to handle snakes from others in his area. Because he lived in a rural area, he may have learned to charm them out of necessity, or it may have been for more religious reasons" (Simmons and Ogden 119).

Like snakes, alligators, and tales about alligators, are plentiful in Florida. Kevin M. McCarthy recently compiled an entire collection of stories, appropriately titled *Alligator Tales*, about these creatures in Florida. One tall tale about alligators was told by Cracker pioneer Ted Smallwood from Chokoloskee. He says that Thomas Roberts (who has a lake named after him) went hunting in 1898 after a dry spell and found the lake that bears his name "teeming with alligators." After fetching a few friends and some salt to tan the hides, he was able to harvest ten thousand alligators' hides to sell in Fort Meyers.[6]

These kinds of tales read much like the ubiquitous fishing tales. There are also many tales about alligator wrestling, which have sometimes been linked to the Seminoles. However, Bucavalas and others claim that while the Seminoles did take it up in later years, alligator wrestling began with Crackers. In fact, Allen Jumper of Hollywood Reservation stated that the practice was against tribal customs but that the money earned by participating in the performance persuaded them to get involved (Bucuvalas, Bulger, and Kennedy 218–19).

There is no doubt that the alligator attracts attention. The animal has eighty-two teeth, and when it closes its jaws on an object, it exerts nearly two thousand pounds of pressure. This information might make anyone think twice, but couple this with the fact that alligators have extremely small brains; they forget that they have eaten almost ten seconds after a meal! In 1974, there were 4,914 complaints against alligators. This increased to 13,615 complaints by 1995 (Goss 78). If you live in Florida, and you yourself don't have a story about an alligator encounter, you can be sure one of your neighbors does.

This book's title story is an alligator story. While the version in this book lists the Blue Sink as the home of alligator/ex-slave Uncle Monday, other versions claim that he lives in Eatonville's Lake Belle. Collected by Zora Neale Hurston, this legend tells about a powerful Black man who made African medicine and fought with the Seminoles. He waits at the bottom of the lake for a better day.

UNCLE MONDAY

Zora Neale Hurston (1891–1960) was a writer, folklorist, and anthropologist. Eatonville, Florida, was her hometown, and it was this historic town that inspired the creation of many of the characters for her short stories and books. She is best known for her novel, Their Eyes Were Watching God, *published in 1937.*

She did folklore fieldwork in Florida in the 1920s and 1930s. This tale was collected in the 1930s and is still told in Central Florida today.

IN HIS NATIVE AFRICA, Uncle Monday was a big medicine man—a leader in the powerful crocodile cult of men who claimed brotherhood with the savage reptiles. Captured and brought to America as a slave, Uncle Monday soon escaped and made his way from South Carolina and Georgia down into the Indian territory of Florida. There he made strong medicine among the Seminoles and their friends from the West Indies. When the White men banded together to drive the Indians ever deeper into the peninsula, Uncle Monday led the tribesmen in retaliation. They made a last, desperate stand on the shores of Lake Maitland, but were again defeated by superior arms and numbers.

Uncle Monday then led his remaining warriors into the dense woods around Blue Sink Lake. He told them the gods had revealed to him that further resistance to the White men would be useless. But Uncle Monday swore that he would never submit to slavery or death at the hands of the Whites. He said he would change himself into an alligator and join his brother reptiles in the Blue Sink until the wars were over. Then he would come forth from the lake and walk the land in peace.

So the tribe held a ceremony on the banks of the Blue Sink. As the men beat African and Indian rhythms on their drums, Uncle Monday danced. As he danced, his face grew long and terrible, his arms and legs grew shorter, his skin grew thick and scaly, and his voice changed to thunder. From the Blue Sink came an answering roar of deep-throated bellows, and a thousand gators swept up from the lake in a double column. Uncle Monday was the biggest alligator of them all, and he marched majestically between their ranks and slid into the Blue Sink. With a mighty roar, all the other alligators plunged after him.

That's how Uncle Monday changed himself into an alligator. He still lives in the Blue Sink but, every now and then, he changes himself back into a man and walks through the land casting all sorts of spells on folks.

Not long ago, old Judy Bronson of nearby Maitland was bragging around that Uncle Monday wasn't no better Vodou doctor than what she was. She said she could not only undo any spell he cast, but she could throw it right back on him. When Uncle Monday heard about her bragging, all he said was, "The foolishness of tongues is higher than mountains."

Then one day, Judy asked her grandson to rig up a pole and dig some worms for her; she was going fishing down at the Blue Sink, even if the mosquitoes and red-bugs did eat her old carcass up. Folks tried to get her not to go, because Blue Sink is bottomless a few feet from shore; but Judy said she just had to go, and that's all there was to it. She got there at sundown and had no sooner got her hook baited and in the water than she felt the dark slipping up and grabbing hold of her like a varmint.

Judy wanted to get up and run off through the brush, but her legs were paralyzed. Then she heard a big wind coming rushing across the brush, and the next thing she knew, she had fallen into the Blue Sink. Of all things on earth, Judy was most afraid of the dark and the water and now they both had her in their claws. She was afraid to move for fear she might slip off into the deep. Finally, she found strength enough to scream, and at the sound of her voice, a bright beam of light fell across the Blue Sink like a flaming sword, pointing straight at her.

Then Judy saw Uncle Monday. He was clad in flowing robes and marched across the water toward her. Behind him swam an army of gators.

"I brought you here," said Uncle Monday, "and here you will stay until you own up that you can't do no such magic as me."

The light faded, and Uncle Monday and the gators sank beneath the water. But one big gator remained, and settled up so close to Judy she couldn't help touching him when she breathed.

Judy hated like everything to give way to Uncle Monday, but she was too scared to let pride stand in her way. First, she admitted it inside, and then she said it out loud. When she did, the alligator swam off into the darkness, and she heard her grandson calling to her. Soon, she was lifted out of the Blue Sink and carried home.

Folks still try to tell Judy that she only suffered a stroke and fell in the lake, but she knows better. She threw away all her Vodou potions, bottles, and equipment. She now says she has Uncle Monday to thank for being able to walk again. And she never questions Uncle Monday's medicine.

Such is the living power of Uncle Monday in the land around the Blue Sink. Sometimes, he walks through the countryside as a man, but he always changes into an alligator again and returns to the Blue Sink. When he does, all the other alligators in the lake keep up an all-night bellowing, and folks in the village hear them and breathe a sigh of relief. You see, both the alligators and the people living around Blue Sink feel much more comfortable with Uncle Monday home in the waters with his reptile family.

REFLECTIONS: *Can you tell which parts of this tale are based in history? What does this story teach you about the Seminole wars and the Seminoles? Can you describe what it must be like to live by Lake Maitland based on this tale?*

HOW TO HANDLE A RATTLESNAKE

Reptiles have always had a certain appeal to storytellers. It is fitting that Florida would have tales about snakes since they are so plentiful in the state. Like stories about alligator wrestlers, tales about individuals who can handle or tame snakes are of special interest to those who live alongside these dangerous reptiles.

Someone who knew Ole Man Davis and had watched him with the snakes told this tale, which was then recorded in the 1930s. Some independent Pentecostal Holiness churches in the South used poisonous snakes in their worship based on their reading of Mark 16:18, which says, "They shall take up serpents." Ole Man Davis may have been associated with this practice. If so, perhaps this rattlesnake tamer believed that faith would protect him.

OLE MAN DAVIS was a large, powerful man who served as the caretaker of a herd of cattle. The cattle owner lived in a Swiss chalet on the St. Johns River in Switzerland, Florida. During the early 1960s Ole Man Davis lived with his wife and a half a dozen tow-headed children in a barn-like structure on State Road 13 across from the chalet. The owner of the chalet operated a meat market in Jacksonville Beach, and Ole Man Davis brought home the scrap meat which had been thrown out, boiled it as one does to sterilize hop slop obtained from similar sources, and raised his family on it. His home, situated as it was in the middle of the cattle herd, had flies all around it.

"Just some of the flies we raise around here," he would say tolerantly as he brushed the swarms away from his eyes. He almost thought of them as members of his family.

Davis embodied as much human dignity as I ever saw in any one human. He reminded me of Theodore Roosevelt and some of those portraits of those other early Presidents, only more so.

Davis knew an awful lot about Nature and stuff like that. For instance, I had a solitary yellow pine on my property down the road that was about five feet in diameter. There was nothing like it for miles around. Davis looked up at the top of that ole pine tree and said, "Reason it's so big, is because it has a bleedin' heart."

Bleedin' heart, it turns out, means hollow inside. Davis could tell by a bit of moss piled up at the top. This kind of moss grows only around holes, he said.

He knew about all kinds of things like that.

I'd often drive him down Roberts Road, which was a one-lane dirt trail in those days. We'd be going about fifty miles an hour, and he would suddenly holler, "Stop the car!"

When that happened, it was usually because he had seen where a rattlesnake had left a trail in the sand crossing the road. You see, he knew practically all of the rattlesnakes in that area by their first names, and what "gopher" hole they inhabited. He also knew what time of the day each rattlesnake would cross the road to get a drink of water. He knew because he was in the business of catching them and selling them to Ross Allen, a herpetologist (that's a reptile specialist). Ross Allen lived in Silver Springs. When he got the rattlesnakes he "milked" their fangs for venom to produce antitoxin (that's medicine for people bit by poisonous snakes).

One time he told me how to cut a hickory switch and tickle a rattlesnake under its throat with it. Davis explained that "for a while that rattlesnake will strike at the stick all he can, but after a while he becomes ashamed of himself and tries to hide his head under his own body. Then you can pick him up and do anything you want with him. He won't bite you."

I laughed and laughed, which hurt his feelings. But then some weeks later, when I was at his place, he said, "You laughed when I told you about how to handle a rattlesnake. Come over here. I want to show you something."

Davis had a six-foot rattler in the bottom of a barrel all coiled and ready to strike anything that came within reach. He cut himself a switch, and started tickling.

Things began to happen just as he said they would. The rattler finally stopped rattling and tucked his head under his body, Davis reached in and lifted him out by the back of the neck. The rattler was real laid-back. He didn't twitch or squirm at all. He just hung out his full length and Davis proceeded to drape him around his arms, waist, and neck. There was no threat at all. His children and I stood around and stared. It was one of the most amazing things I've ever seen.

For all I know, this may be the secret of all the snake-handling groups in the South. Those preachers may all know what Ole Man Davis knows. Somebody might be out back of the pulpit, out of sight, tickling those rattlers. You might want to check it out, but take care. If you get bit, don't say I put you up to it.

REFLECTIONS: *Can you tell this story from the rattlesnake's point-of-view? Describe what they see, like, and know about the land they live in. Explain how they view their relationship with Ole Man Davis.*

OLD PETE

In the days before the Industrial Revolution, people had to use their muscles in their work more than they do today. Now we have machines that do much of the lifting and hauling for us. But back then, having strong people around to do difficult work was important. The stories about these muscular individuals are still told today.

This legend will remind some readers of Paul Bunyan and John Henry, also extremely strong men who embodied the work ethic and challenged the machine. Stories about Paul Bunyan eventually entered into the poetry of Robert Frost and Carl Sandburg, and many songs were written about John Henry. A major theme of these legends is the same in all cases: a discomfort with machines that might displace human laborers.

MOST PEOPLE WHO enjoy folktales are familiar with the exploits of Louisiana's John Henry and Minnesota's Paul Bunyan. They were both incredibly strong men who helped build the United States in the early days.

But it is not so well known that for many years West Florida had a renowned character in real life similar to John Henry. He was "Old Pete," an African American man who died at Port Tampa in 1934, at the age of sixty-seven. Old Pete's amazing feats and whopping stories rival the marvelous accomplishments of John Henry and Paul Bunyan.

The tales about Old Pete's incredible strength are many. Once he used a ship anchor for a pickax. He lifted a derailed locomotive back onto the track. He swam out into the ocean and pushed a grounded ship off a sandbar back into deep waters. And one time he pulled up a big tree by the roots, toted it home on his back and cut it up into three cords of firewood.

His real name was Henry Peterson, but he was generally known simply as "Pete." When he got old, he was "Old Pete." Many residents of Port Tampa, where he spent the last twenty years of his life, remember his strong figure, cheerful grin, and religious enthusiasm. But more vivid is the memory of his reputation for remarkable physical powers and as a teller of astounding and amusing tales.

In his younger days, Pete had been a giant of a man. He was stronger than anyone around, and he had a splendid physique. Even at the time of his death he was still vigorous and mentally alert. Born in slavery, he had worked at various times as a plantation hand, dock laborer, railroad worker, and sawmill hand. At the time of his death, he was a laborer at the Atlantic Coast Line railroad shops at Port Tampa. He had lived and worked in many sections of Florida.

Pete was said to have a skull an inch thick and as hard as iron. Old Port Tampa residents vouch for the story that he would engage in a butting match with any billy goat for fifty cents a match and that Pete always won. In a butting contest Pete would get down on his hands and knees and meet the goat "head on." Their heads would come together with a resounding "whack." The battle and clash of skulls would continue until the goat finally walked off defeated, shaking his whiskers with humiliation. Pete would grin and pocket the winner's fee of "four bits."

Old-time residents of Port Tampa tell of the time a freight car ran over Pete's head, with no damage except to the car. As the story goes, Pete had gone to sleep beside the track in the car repair shed, using one of the rails as a pillow. A switch engine "kicked" a car into the shed for repairs. The front wheels passed bumpily over his cranium, but the hard skull derailed the rear tracks. Some workmen nearby saw it and rushed to pick up the supposed dead body. Pete was still sound asleep and snoring! When they woke him and informed him what had happened, the sleepy

man rubbed his eyes, felt his head, and drowsily remarked, "Doggone! My head does feel kinda funny."

Pete often helped unload cargoes of coconuts that came into Port Tampa on ships from Honduras. For a nickel he would allow anyone to smash a coconut on his head. But this was just one of his minor stunts.

One of Pete's feats of strength was stopping a runaway freight train by the sheer strength of his big body. As Pete told it, one of the six freight cars got loose in the railroad yards and rolled down the mile-long grade to the dock. It was about to run into the bay. Pete, who happened to be at the dock, saw it coming. He sprang to the middle of the track, faced the advancing car, and braced himself. With back bowed and hands outstretched, he waited. As the car came against his hands he braced and pushed. It forced him back, but he kept on bracing and pushing. Finally, within three feet of the dock's edge, he stopped the runaway car. Then he gave it a mighty shove forward, and it rolled back up into the yards again!

Pete was not only strong, he was brave. Once, while working for a farmer ten miles from Fort Myers, he was sent to town to bring back a mule his employer had purchased there. Pete set out to walk to Fort Myers, carrying a saddle and bridle, so that he could ride the mule back to the farm. On his way through a swampy woods, he saw an alligator. Pete captured the gator, saddled and bridled him, jumped on his back with a whip, and made the scaly steed carry him at a gallop to Fort Myers. There he sold the gator to a circus for ten dollars, transferred the saddle and bridle to the mule, and rode back to the farm.

Another time, Pete was a deck passenger on an old stern-wheel steamboat going to Jacksonville. The steamer's crankshaft broke, and the captain announced that the accident would cause a twenty-four-hour delay in reaching the city. But Pete was in a hurry, so he grabbed the crank and began to turn the paddlewheel himself. He turned it so fast that the boat got to Jacksonville three hours ahead of its regular schedule.

It is hard to imagine that John Henry or Paul Bunyan was any stronger or braver than Old Pete. No way it could happen. Even today, Florida residents tell the tales of Old Pete, the strongest, most amazing hero of them all.

REFLECTIONS: *Who is the strongest person you know? What kind of stories can you tell about his or her strength? What would happen if you exaggerated those stories? Would they be more fun to tell and hear?*

RAILROAD BILL

In many African American stories, Blacks are depicted as being adept at moving through the landscape, a skill that is often needed when on the run. In this legend, Railroad Bill is not only able to escape being caught by knowing how and where to hide, he is able to change into an animal or a tree in order to elude the sheriff and his men. In storytelling, giving the underdog certain powers makes for a more even play-ing field and gives the character a chance to win at the game. It is fitting that Bill has the power to change into a fox, which is a sly and cunning creature.

Railroad Bill is a folk outlaw. Our most famous Robin Hood–like outlaws are usually advocates for their communities, as is the case here. Railroad Bill, like many other outlaws, steals from the rich and gives to the poor. These characters are often forced into hiding by an injustice or minor crime, and they kill only in self-defense or to even the score.

AN ELDERLY BLACK WOMAN opened the door of her unpainted shack, which was set back from the sandy road leading to Piney Grove near the Florida-Alabama line. On one of the splintered steps of the porch she found a stack of canned goods. She knew Railroad Bill had put them there during the night. She also knew they were stolen from an L & N boxcar. The woman understood that Bill should not have taken the canned goods, but she was mighty hungry. Without these canned foods, she would not eat.

The Escambia County sheriff had been chasing Bill for five years, but he would always escape. One time, the sheriff and his men took a train to a place where they thought Bill was hiding, but the elusive thief stayed in another car on the same train and loaded his sack with more plunder.

On another occasion, the sheriff's men followed Bill to an area where they had not searched before. When the hunters looked in a cluster of bushes, they chased a red fox from its hiding place. They shot, but the little red fox turned around and laughed at them in a high, wild, hearty roar. The old Black woman knew the fox was Railroad Bill. He had a way of turning himself into an animal or a tree.

The five year chase leading to the arrest of Railroad Bill started shortly after the

War Between the States when a man the White folks knew as Morris Slater refused to register the rifle he carried while hunting. Slater, a Black man, was then living in Bluff Springs where he worked for Bradford's Turpentine Company. When the sheriff had accosted Slater and told him to register the gun, Slater quickly walked away. One of the men shot at him but missed. Slater found shelter in a swamp near the railroad tracks. In order to survive he robbed trains. The L & N officials in Montgomery hired detectives to track down the man who was now thought of as dangerous. He had exchanged shots with a railroad flagman and had also killed an Alabama lawman.

The hunt continued. Sheriff McMillan led a party to Bluff Springs. Railroad Bill, hiding behind a tree, saw the party coming and promptly shot the sheriff. One of the sheriff's men fired several rounds at the Black man and thought he had killed the elusive Bill. Not wishing to retrieve the Black man's body at night, the sheriff's men left the scene. Next morning there was no sign of Railroad Bill, only the tree where he had been.

Bill finally met his end in Atmore, Alabama. The well-built bandit was sitting on a barrel eating crackers and cheese when Constable McGowan shot and killed him. When the body was searched authorities found his Winchester rifle concealed in the left pant leg and a loaded pistol in the belt. Railroad Bill's body was laid out on a packing crate. Bitterweeds were placed in his mouth.

His legend continues. African American folk songs about Bill were composed and passed on to the next generation. Many Blacks did not believe he was dead. When the federal government sent food commodities into the area during the Great Depression, many people believed the spirit of Railroad Bill had sent them.

REFLECTIONS: *How is this legend like the story of "Robin Hood," and how is it different? What parts of this story do you think are based in fact? What can you learn about history by studying this legend?*

BONE MIZELL AND HIS TEETH

Bone Mizell, one of Florida's early Cracker cowboys, was a real person who was born in 1863 and died in 1921. He worked the early cattle industry in South Florida. Jim Bob Tinsley, from Ocala, is the best-known teller of Bone Mizell tales. In 1990 he published a book on Bone Mizell titled Florida Cow Hunter: The Life and Times of Bone Mizell. *He reports that Bone was "about six feet tall, rawboned and tanned to the color of a new saddle." Bone was a generous man who was known for his wild spending sprees. Never caring to be wealthy, he sometimes stoked his pipe with paper money. He drank too much and was often in trouble with the law. Today he is known as the King of all Cowmen.*

This story is one of Jim Bob Tinsley's best legends about Bone Mizell.

ONE DAY I WAS riding the range with Buck King, the boss, and Bone. We discovered a thin old cow at the edge of a thicket of thornbush. She was a quarrelsome old beast, evidently planning on taking on Bone and get the best of him. Buck challenged Bone: "Rope her and put your mark on her, and you can have her." Bone accepted the challenge and soon had rope on the cow's horns. He dismounted quickly, with knife in hand, but the old cow was hard to handle. She dragged Bone into the thicket, where he lost his knife and had most of his clothes ripped off by the thorny scrub. He finally emerged, a sorry spectacle, dragging his lariat. King chided him on being bested by an old range cow.

"But I put my mark on her," declared Bone.

"How could you mark her? I saw you lose your knife," answered King.

"Marked her with my teeth—just as good as I could have done it with a knife," declared Bone.

We ran the old cow out of the brush and sure enough, Bone's claim was clear as day—he had put his mark in her ears with his teeth.

REFLECTIONS: *Have you heard other stories about someone this fearless? Do you think Bone Mizell was a brave cowboy, and do you think he really knew how to handle cattle? Why would he behave in this manner? Do you admire him or not? Why?*

BONE MIZELL AND THE CIRCUS

Bone Mizell was famous for many reasons. One reason is because the famous nine-teenth-century artist Frederic Remington sketched Bone on his horse with his dog by his side when he was in Arcadia in 1895. Remington was interested in Florida's fron-tier and its cowmen, and Bone Mizell was the perfect model. It is said that after Bone posed for the artist, Remington paid him with a drink.

This is another Jim Bob Tinsley tale about Bone Mizell, the cowboy who worked the early ranches in South Florida.

BONE MIZELL WAS A prankster of a cowboy. He was always making practical jokes. He didn't seem to care how he might have to pay for his actions.

Now when a traveling show came to town, it was an event sure to be attended by a large crowd. But Bone often stole the limelight from the performers. When the circus came to Arcadia and set up next to the railroad tracks, he got into trouble for capturing the audience's attention and was escorted from the tent by circus officials. Once outside, Bone untied a tent rope and attached it to a freight train stopped nearby. As the train pulled out, it effectively took the circus with it. The next morning Bone was fined seventy-five dollars, but he didn't resent the penalty. He said the prank was worth an even thousand bucks to him—including nine hundred and twenty-five dollars in personal satisfaction to see the show leave town the way it did.

REFLECTIONS: *What would make Bone Mizell do such a thing? Can you describe what happened to the acrobats, clowns, and animals in the circus tent?*

ACREFOOT JOHNSON

Many people like to tell stories about Acrefoot Johnson, Florida's legendary barefoot mailman. Frog Smith, a well-known Cracker writer from Saint Petersburg, told stories about him in the early 1900s, and Will McLean, one of Florida's great singer/songwriters, sang about him. This version of the tale comes from Phyllis NeSmith, a contemporary teller of tales.

Although the origin of many legends is obscure, this story situates the hero in a specific time and place. As it is told over and over again, the story develops and expands.

I COME FROM a little ole place called Nocatee, which is in Southwest Florida. And that's where this story took place back in the 1880s. It's about a fellow you might of heard of; his name was Acrefoot Johnson. The Barefoot Mailman. It's no wonder he was called that. He wore a size fourteen shoe—when he wore shoes at all, which was seldom!

He was six feet seven inches tall, with the longest legs you ever saw, and he had a mail route that stretched from Fort Meade to Fort Ogden—about sixty-five miles. He walked that route, barefoot, three times a week, carrying the mail on his back. He walked so fast that horses had to trot to keep up with him.

The story goes that one day Acrefoot was getting ready to set out from the Fort Meade post office, when Ziba King came by. Now Ziba just happened to be a judge and one of the richest ranchers in that part of the country. He was on his way home to Fort Ogden with his new horse, pulling his brand new buggy. Ziba was right proud of that rig. He swore that he now had the fastest rig in the country.

Feeling in a benevolent mood, Ziba called, "Hey there, Acrefoot! Just got this new rig, and I'll be glad to give you a lift to Fort Ogden. Hop in!"

Acrefoot looked over at Ziba, finished filling that big bag of his, hoisted it up on his back, and then strolled over and carefully examined both the buggy and that fine new horse.

Finally, he said, "It is a fine rig, Judge, and I'd like a rain check on your offer, but I'm in a kind of hurry today," and he turned and headed down that dirt road.

Ziba decided to take Acrefoot down a notch or two. He tore off down that road after him. The judge was sure that even if Acrefoot took the shortest route possible—just like the crow flies—even if Acrefoot went through creeks, palmettos, pine woods, brambles, whatever, with his new rig, this would be one race that Acrefoot would lose.

Several hours later, Ziba came tearing up to the post office in Fort Ogden in a cloud of dust. That fine new horse of his was in a lather and the buggy was covered with grime, but Ziba had a big grin on his face because he knew he had won. But—there sat Acrefoot! That's right! There sat Acrefoot on the steps of the post office with an even bigger grin on *his* face. He looked over at Ziba and said, "What took ya so long?"

REFLECTIONS: *What do you think a mail carrier's life would be like in the 1880s? Do you think Acrefoot enjoyed his work? Why do you think Acrefoot had the power to outrun the horse and buggy?*

THE TURKEY MAIDEN

There are many recognizable aspects to this tale, including the wicked stepmother, the three wishes, the magic nuts, the journey, invisibility, the lowly young girl who marries the prince, and magic clothing. Dwarfs often appear in folktales as magicians, and in this case the dwarf was connected to the magic nuts. The nuts help the heroine in reversing her fortune, which is connected to an ancient belief in amulets. In every culture, there are tales about magic journeys. This kind of traveling is always about some kind of transformation or life change. Magic clothes are also found in numerous folk tales and can be thought of as revealing a hidden persona through the use of a mask, or a shaman-like covering. The number three appears often in European-based folktales, as it is used here with the three wishes granted by the nuts, whereas the number four is prevalent in Native American folklore.

"The Turkey Maiden" is a Spanish tale told to Ralph Steel Boggs in the Ybor City area in the 1930s. Maria Redmon recently translated it.

ONCE UPON A TIME there was a widower who had a daughter. He fell in love with a widow who had two daughters, and they soon married. The widower's daughter, whose name was Rosa, was mistreated by her stepsisters and stepmother. One day she decided she could take the mistreatment no longer and would leave home and live on her own. Her father was very sad, but could see that his daughter was determined to leave. Before she left, her father gave her a gift of three nuts, and he told her that whenever she was in danger she should break open one of the nuts, and she would be protected. Then they kissed and said good-bye.

Rosa walked for a long time. She went from town to town, looking for work. One day, while she was walking through the forest, she noticed some men were following her. She became very frightened and broke open one of the nuts. To her surprise, from inside the nut appeared a dress made of wood. She put on the dress, which made her invisible in the forest of trees. And so she was saved from the danger in the woods and eagerly continued on her way.

One day, feeling very hungry and cold, she decided to open another nut. Suddenly there appeared before her a dwarf that only she could see.

"And what do you want, Miss Rosa?" said the dwarf.

She was so surprised that it took her a long time to tell the dwarf how hungry and cold she was. In a flash Rosa had the best food and warm fire before her. Of course, the dwarf was magical and could do all of these things.

She continued on her journey, and the dwarf accompanied her. Finally they arrived at a beautiful palace. The dwarf told her to go to the palace and ask for work. She did as he asked, and she was given work caring for the turkeys because she looked like an honest girl.

The dwarf told her that every day at sunset she should say:

Turkey, Turkey,
Oh, if only the king's son were to fall in love with me!

And every evening, as the sun set, she would say:

Turkey, Turkey,
Oh, if only the king's son were to fall in love with me!

And the Turkeys would answer:

Yes, yes, yes!
Gobble, gobble, gobble!

And one of the turkeys would die. No one noticed that the turkeys were missing until one day the king, looking at the fields from his palace, saw that there were not as many turkeys as before, and he wanted to know why. Then one day he looked at the field where the turkey maiden had been, and he saw nothing. Every day afterwards was the same.

One day the king's son arrived from school, and as he was inspecting his father's lands, he saw Rosa dressed in her dress of wood. He thought she looked strange in a dress of wood, but he said nothing and continued on his way. Rosa fell in love with him at once, but she was very sad, because she knew that the prince did not love her. The dwarf saw that she was sad and told her to make a dress of flowers and to dance, because it was springtime. She did as he asked, and one day the king saw her as he looked at the field. He thought she was a fairy, so every day he looked for her. The prince saw her too, and he fell in love with her. No one realized that this fairy was really the turkey maiden.

One day the prince fell ill, and none of the doctors could cure him, because his illness was of the heart. The dwarf told Rosa to go to the king and tell him that she could cure the prince. She did as the dwarf had told her, but no one would let her see the prince. Finally, seeing that the prince was not getting better, the king decided to allow the girl to see him. While she walked through the magnificent hallways, she thought of how she looked. She decided to open the third nut and from it appeared a beautiful dress. She put it on immediately. When they arrived at the prince's room, and he saw her, he began to feel better. He told her that he loved her with all his heart, and that he wanted to marry her. She told him that she also loved him, and so, they soon were married and lived happily ever after.

This tale is finished and yours has just begun.

REFLECTIONS: *Magic clothes are used in numerous folktales. Can you name three? Do you have any clothes that make you feel powerful or different? Can you tell a story about them?*

4

Food, Friends, and Family

Just about everyone tells stories about food, friends, and family. These tales are part of our everyday experiences. When these stories get repeated often, they become folktales.

Before the Industrial Revolution, people lived in multigenerational units often including in-laws, aunts, and uncles.[1] This was true in Florida for a wide variety of ethnic groups. Family groups would gather together in the evenings, around the dinner table and in the living room, to entertain informally and be entertained with storytelling activities. But the telling of tales also occurred when neighbors and friends got together in more public spaces.

In the Panhandle region of Florida, entertainment centered on common work spaces, the farm and the river, and in gathering places such as the church, school, and in the towns. Because people depended on each other to get many necessary chores accomplished, a collective camaraderie was important to survival. These tasks included barn raisings, hog killings, log rolling and splitting, and cane grindings. Quilting parties and other work gatherings related to food preparation and the home were prevalent for the women. During and after these activities, stories were told to make the tasks more enjoyable. One common activity that still occurs today and is popular with young people is the "pindar" or peanut shellings and boilings. Neighbors meet at a designated place, and, after the work is done, the evening is set aside for entertainment that usually includes games, music, and conversation (McGregory 83–85). Of course good conversation includes storytelling.

African Americans throughout Florida often met in places called joots, jukes, or juke-joints. (In some area, joots are still popular today.) In the early part of the twentieth century these nightly gathering spaces could be as simple as a dance space for young people, or as spicy as a backwoods tavern with illegal gambling, moonshine (known as "white mule"), and active dancing to a nickel phonograph, piano playing, or blues singing. According to folklore fieldwork done on Florida's African American population at this time, if the joot gathering was a nightly event, it was generally small with perhaps two or three dozen people present. It was likely that more men than women would be present, and this unequal distribution of coupling often resulted in fights breaking out. The prevalence of violence caused owners to begin posting signs banning guns and knives (McDonogh 57–58). What happened the night before at a local joot might make for good storytelling material at another place or time.

Residents of rural areas often sought amusement in the city. For African American in the 1930s, this was particularly true in areas like Orlando and Winter Park, where there were numerous farmhands and domestic workers, and in Palatka, which was the center of logging and sawmill activity. These towns offered restaurants, beer gardens, and various other places for men and women to enjoy music, dancing, and lively conversation. These recreational spaces were crowded every night of the week, and it wasn't unusual for people to attend on a regular basis. When the music stopped, remaining party-goers often walked down the street to someone's house to continue the evening's dancing and conversation. This custom was especially intense in Quincy's African American neighborhood and along Tampa's Central Avenue (McDonogh 58). Much swapping of stories must have taken place amongst friends at these spots. Many stories must have been made around these nights out.

Crackers often met at the dry-goods stores in town to swap tales and gossip, debate politics, and talk about the weather and the success or failure of their crops. During these times people from every social class would engage in conversation and dialogue about local events. They would sit on large wooden soda cracker barrels, hence the term "cracker barrel philosopher" (Ste. Claire 104). There were many other social gathering places for Florida Crackers. Getting together with neighbors was important because they were so isolated in Florida's early years. These gatherings, as is true of all of Florida's ethnic and cultural groups, resulted in reinforcing values, beliefs, and a way of life (Ste. Claire 104).

Telling tales helps to maintain relationships among friends and family. It is easy to tell stories to friends and family because they already have some generalized understanding of shared values and belief structures that make the story "work" for those who are listening. Friends and family more readily understand the conversational style that is used. The words we choose and the way we say them are crucial to the understanding of the message, because the way we talk says something about our relationship with others (Tannen). Zora Neale Hurston explained it this way: "Look like to me only a fool would want you to talk in a way that feel peculiar to your mind" (qtd. in Gates viii).

When friends and family come together for entertainment, they often do so around food. Food can be used to unite people, as it does when familiar foods are served, or it can estrange people from each other when the food choices seem foreign (Tokarev). Folklorist Michael Owen Jones wrote about the social aspects of food, claiming that it is both a physiological and an intellectual experience. He observed that "food can enliven social relations, enrich spiritual affairs, and enhance an individual's sense of well-being; it can be used to threaten, reward, cajole, or punish and in other ways manipulate behavior" (Jones 106). Not only is food shared with friends and family a catalyst for storytelling activities, it is also the creative subject matter for traditional tales.

The traditional tales in this section all revolve around food, friends, or family. They are both believable and unbelievable. Incredible things are sometimes made to seem credible. Some of the tales are humorous, and some have serious messages to impart. They are stories we can easily identify with because they deal with people and events that are, in some ways, familiar. Through these stories we can learn more about the importance of food and celebrating with family and friends. We can also, more simply, have a good laugh.

KEROSENE CHARLEY AND THE POTATOES

This African-American tale was collected at the early part of the twentieth century. Food is a common subject matter in traditional tales. There are magic apples that cause deathlike sleep as in "Snow White," the apple from the Garden of Eden that causes trouble in paradise, and the enticing gingerbread house in "Hansel and Gretel." The focus on food, in this case, is humorous. It is a story with which we can all easily identify.

ONE TIME Kerosene Charley got a job digging potatoes. Before he started work in the morning, his bossman gave him a breakfast of fried potatoes. Kerosene Charley didn't much like potatoes, but he didn't say anything, because he was mighty glad to get the job. Besides, he was hungry.

He dug potatoes all morning, and when lunchtime came around he went to the back door of his bossman's house, and the bossman's wife handed him a big plate of boiled potatoes. This made Kerosene Charley pretty mad, but he didn't say anything, because he figured they'd give him a good supper after feeding him potatoes all day.

So he finished up his day's work, and when it came suppertime he could hardly wait to see what he would be served. Well, it turned out to be baked potatoes this time, with a big piece of potato pie for dessert! Kerosene Charley made up his mind to quit that job right then and there, but he was too tired to leave. So he decided to spend the night and leave before it got daylight.

Way in the middle of the night, the bossman heard Kerosene Charley moaning with a bellyache.

"That poor guy is ailing with a bellyache," he said to his wife. "I guess we've got to do something for him. I can't get any sleep with him moaning like that."

"All right," his wife said. "I'll get up and make him some potato tea."

REFLECTIONS: *Why do you think the bossman's wife fed Kerosene Charley so many potatoes instead of something else? Why do some potatoes have "eyes"? Is there some kind of food you have at your house that is served in many different ways? Do you like it more or less because you have it so often? Do some foods taste better only if you have it once in a while? Is there anything you'd like to eat every single day? Was Kerosene Charley just a picky eater?*

THE LITTLE BOY AND THE "AYAYAY"

Liliane Nérette Louis, from Miami, often tells this story, which she heard as a child growing up in Haiti. She explains that her stories suggest ways that children might learn to handle situations in everyday life.

Haitian stories are most often told at night when the family is gathered together. In fact, Louis suggests that it may even be bad luck to tell stories during the day because some mysterious force might "get you." She explains that this superstition may be told to let children know that there are other important things that they should be doing during the day—like going to school. It is also the time when grown-ups have work and chores to do and can't easily take the time to tell stories.

To create the mood and let the audience know it is time to begin, Haitian storytellers say, "Kric," and the audience replies, "Krac." With that response, the story begins. This traditional practice led Liliane Nérette Louis to name her 1999 book of traditional tales When Night Falls, Kric! Krac!

ONE TIME a little boy was living with his aunt, because he had no mommy and no daddy. But the aunt was terrible to him. She used to beat him all the time. No matter what the little boy did, she said it was wrong. The little boy was responsible for almost all the household chores. He would clean, cook, take care of the front and back yards, take water from the river to the house, wash the clothes, and go to the market. Everything was the little boy's responsibility—even killing the chickens! But every day the aunt would find a reason to beat the little boy, no matter how well he thought he did his chores.

One day he worked so hard and so well, the aunt couldn't find any reason to be angry with the little boy. She tried but she couldn't think of any reason to beat the little boy. So she said to him, "I see that you did your work pretty well, but I'm sure I didn't see something you must have done wrong. Now come over here."

The little boy moved closer, afraid of what might happen next.

The aunt continued, "I'm going to send you to the market. I'm sending you to the market to buy some 'ayayay.'"

"Ayayay" in English means "ouch," but the little boy didn't know that. So, the little boy asked, "Auntie what is 'ayayay'? I don't know 'ayayay.'"

The aunt was happy she had the little boy confused. Somewhat scolding, she said, "What do you mean you don't know 'ayayay'? That's the first time I've ever heard that. Somebody who doesn't know what 'ayayay' means? 'Ayayay'—all the time people say 'ayayay' and you don't know what it means? Well, I don't care. I want you to go to the market and get me some 'ayayay.' And if you don't get my 'ayayay,' I will give you a good beating! It will be better you weren't born, because I'm really going to beat you! You better find me that 'ayayay.'"

The little boy left the house crying, crying. He didn't know what to do. He kept asking himself where he could find "ayayay." He didn't even know what "ayayay" was. So he just walked the street crying.

A man was passing by. He said to him, "Little boy, why are you so sad?"

The little boy answered, "Oh sir, it's my aunt who told me to go buy some 'ayayay'! I don't know what 'ayayay' is, and if I don't take the 'ayayay' to her, she going to beat me up very bad."

The man was puzzled. He didn't know how to help. He said, "Oh little boy, I wish I could help you, but I really don't know what 'ayayay' is. You'll have to ask someone else." And he left the boy crying.

The little boy kept on walking. He really didn't know what "ayayay" was, and he didn't know how to find out. Everybody on the street saw him crying. One by one they would ask him how they could help. But no one could tell him where to get some "ayayay."

Then the little boy came upon an old lady. This was a very old lady who had a lot of experience. She saw the little boy crying and called to him, "Come over here, little boy. Why are you crying so much?"

The boy replied, "Oh, it's my auntie. She beats me every day. And today she's going to beat me very hard. She might kill me, because she wants me to buy her some 'ayayay' and I don't know what 'ayayay' is."

This was a very smart old lady who could solve most any problem. So she said, "Little boy, come on. I'll find you some 'ayayay.' Don't you worry. Come over there, let's go over there. Let's go to the ocean."

So, together they went to the ocean, and the old lady picked up four big crabs. Four big fat crabs! And she put them in the little boy's basket. Then she went to the

forest and picked up some pine needles—big long pine needles. And she put the pine needles in the little boy's basket on top of the crabs.

Then she asked the little boy, "Do you have anything else to buy?"

And the little boy answered, "Yes, my aunt wants me to do all the marketing for today."

So the old lady told the boy to go to the market and buy all the fruits and vegetables his aunt wanted. She said to place these things carefully on top of the pine needles. And then she said, "When you get home, tell your auntie that the 'ayayay' is in the bottom of the basket, and she should put her hand all the way down to get it. Don't worry, she should be very happy, because that's where the 'ayayay' is."

So, the little boy did exactly what the old lady told him. He went to the market, bought rice, peas, vegetables, and lettuce—everything that his aunt told him to buy. Then he went back home. He was no longer crying. In fact, he felt very happy.

When he got home, the aunt saw him looking satisfied, so she asked, "Why are you so happy? Don't you know that I'm going to beat you up for the 'ayayay' that you haven't found?"

To her surprise, the little boy said, "Oh no, Auntie, I found your 'ayayay.'"

The aunt was very surprised. She knew this was impossible, but she said, "Oh, so you found my 'ayayay'? Well then, come over here, and let me see what the 'ayayay' is. And if it's not 'ayayay,' you better be prepared, because I'm going to beat you up!"

The little boy was pretty sure of himself, so he agreed. "Okay, Auntie, I'm sure I found you your 'ayayay.' Put your hands all the way in the basket, and you can pick up the 'ayayay.'"

So, the auntie did just what the little boy told her to do. She was in such a hurry to find that "ayayay" that she put her hands all the way down to the bottom of the basket.

And—OOF!! "'AYAYAY'!!" she cried. "'AYAYAY'!! 'AYAYAY'!!"

Two of the big crabs were biting hard at her hands and blood was coming out. She yelled so loud that everybody in the village came to see what the excitement was all about. Everybody came, even the sheriff. And when they heard the story that she was the one who asked for the "ayayay," they believed she got what she asked for. But it also became clear to the villagers that she had treated the little boy very badly. And ever since that day when the aunt discovered the "ayayay," she stopped beating the little boy, because the sheriff and the villagers watched her and the little boy very carefully. Because of the "ayayay," the little boy was a lot happier.

REFLECTIONS: *What else could the little boy have put in the basket that might be "ayayay"? Can you make up another ending to this story? Would it make a difference what kind of creature you put in the basket? Why are some people so mean? Did the little boy do a good job of handing a mean person?*

GRANDPA AND THE PANTHER

This is a story that is told by many storytellers around Florida. This version comes from Will McLean (1919–1990), one of Florida's most famous singer/songwriters and storytellers. He is so well known that a Florida festival takes place in his honor each year, and in 1996 he was celebrated by being inducted into the Florida Artists Hall of Fame.

McLean would often lead into his songs by telling stories about Florida. Often he personalized the tales. It is not unusual for storytellers to tell a story they heard from someone else as if the event happened to a member of their family. In this case, the family member is a grandfather. Numerous storytellers have also told this tale about fathers, brothers, uncles, and other relatives and friends.

MY GRANDFATHER, as a young man, left his home place in Alabama and took up land on Holmes Creek in North Florida. There he built his house and sired his young ones. Sweet potatoes, corn, beans, squash, and greens were the usual fare served at the table. Ribbon, green and red cane gave syrup and sugar while blueberry, plum and blackberry gave jam and jelly. Following bees to the bee tree, cutting it down, and filling wooden tubs and buckets with wild honey was a joyful event. Smoke from smoldering old rags wrapped around sticks made the bees sleepy, but if someone did get stung, there was always a snuff dumper in the crowd to rub snuff on the hurt place. Cured meats hung from rafters in the smokehouse on loops of bear grass. Barrels of pickled meats stood against the walls and corners, and sausages hung serpent-like from hickory poles. Holmes Creek teemed with small pike, and other eatable fish were also easily caught. Flour was a luxury. And the infrequent smells of bacon were mouth-watering.

Grandpa cut and rafted logs downriver to a sawmill, and he traded them for hard money. Then he'd walk back along the river's bank. At times, he'd be away from his family for a week, camping and cooking near where he cut the logs. But come noontime Saturday, all work would stop, and he'd pack up, headed for home. This Saturday at noon, Grandpa gathered up his belongings, put them in a tote sack, and moved along. Along about mid-afternoon, he came to a footbridge several hundred feet long, built above the high water line, and over the boggy swamp, across a river to dry land, on the other side. As he neared the part of the bridge that spanned the river, he heard a noise behind him. Turning around quickly, he beheld a huge panther looking at him coming down the bridge toward him. He swung the sack from his shoulder and threw it down on the bridge as close to the panther as he could and started running. The panther proceeded to rip the contents of his sack to pieces. When he finished, he took out after Grandpa. Grandpa was picking up his feet and laying them down. Upon glancing behind him, he saw the panther gaining, and

along comes Grandpa's coat, and on the ground it goes. The panther stops and rips the coat to shreds. Next comes the shirt, and it gets the same treatment. By this time Grandpa's in hollering distance of his house, and he's hollering for Grandma. He jumps a picket fence, grabs a shotgun from Grandma's hand, and as the Panther leaps the fence, puts a load of buckshot in the Panther's face and chest.

That night the Lord blessed Grandma with a life who grew up and became my mother. And for several years after this foot race, Grandpa toted his gun.

Years passed. Grandpa sold his homestead, resettling on a choice piece of land south of Chipley, Florida, not too far from Falling Water. There he built his home, dug his well, and sowed his seed.

REFLECTIONS: *Have you ever heard a story before that's almost just like another story, but a little different too? Can you tell this story, changing it somewhat, as if it happened to someone in your family?*

SISTER'S MILKCOW

Richard Seaman told this tall tale to an audience at the 1992 Florida Folk Festival in White Springs. Born in 1904, Seaman grew up in Central Florida's farming and ranching community. He later moved to Jacksonville. Richard Seaman is a well-known fiddler and storyteller. He learned to play the fiddle by ear when he was ten by attending local square dances. Being a good listener also worked to enhance his ability to tell tales, for a good storyteller is also a good listener.

Folklorist Gregory Hansen reports that Richard Seaman tells his tall tales in a droll style, a typical tall-tale storytelling technique.

MY SISTER had a cow that fell in the well down there one day. The best milk cow they had in Osceola County.

So we went to her place to see about it.

Well, we went down there, and sure enough, the cow was in the well.

At first we didn't know what we were going to do about the cow in the well. Nobody could get it out—in those days we didn't have wreckers or anything to pull them out with in an old abandoned well out there in the field.

Then I told them it wouldn't be any trouble to get the cow out of the well.

So I went into the house, and I got a ladder, and I climbed down the well where the cow was. And I started milking. Well I milked that old cow, and I kept right on milking her.

And I floated her right on out of that well.

There was no trouble to it at all!

REFLECTIONS: *Can you continue the story? What did they do with all that milk in the well? Did they use it instead of water? What would life be like if milk was used instead of water?*

CUTTING A PUMPKIN

This is another tall tale from Richard Seaman. It could also be called a "whopper," or a "tale of lying." Some people might simply refer to it as a lie.

ONE DAY, a neighbor boy came up to the house and asked my dad could he borrow a cross-cut saw. In those days we didn't have chainsaws.

My dad says, "Yes, son, what do you want it for?"

The neighbor replies, "We want to cut a pumpkin."

My dad says, "Well it will be some time this afternoon before you can get it. We're just halfway through a sweet potato."

REFLECTIONS: *What kind of sweet potato could that have been? How big do you think pumpkins can get? Do you think this was as big as Cinderella's pumpkin?*

HOMER AND THE BEAR

Many of Florida's traditional stories are called Cracker tales, because they are about rural Floridians of Anglo-Celtic ancestry. This family story is told by Ada Forney, a storyteller from Melbourne. It is very descriptive, and one can learn much about Florida's environment and Cracker foodways by hearing it.

SOME TIME AGO, my great-grandfather J. J. Lewis and his oldest son, Homer, who was almost ten, went out to fish the evening tide as the sun set over the Indian River. They were out to catch some fish for the northern markets and some mullet for their Thanksgiving dinner. You see, we Florida Crackers don't eat turkey and stuffing like them folks up north do. We have fried mullet, corn muffins, baked beans and coleslaw for our feast. As most Crackers know, mullet are best when caught in the winter months around Thanksgiving. That is when they are spawning, and the fish are many times larger in size than at any other time. This also allows the roe, or fish eggs, to be cooked up and served along with the fish. Ah, fresh Florida caviar! Plus, as Crackers worth their salt also know, mullet are vegetarians and they have a gizzard. So those gizzards get cleaned, wrapped in corn meal and fried in bacon grease along with the fish and roe.

J. J. always took Homer along because Homer could cast a net so perfectly that the weights delicately kissed the water, and before those fish knew what was happening, they were caught. He was better at it than most of the grown men.

It was one of those rare, early cold spells, and the wind was cool and crisp as it blew across the river. Homer was only a kid of a boy, as he liked to say. On this day, as he went to cast the net, he lost his balance and fell overboard. The boy soon broke out in chills and began to turn blue. J. J. rowed him to shore, found a small clearing and built a fire.

"Son, you go strip off those wet clothes while I clean and cook some of these mullet you got with that cast net," J. J. told him. While Homer obeyed, J. J. cut and trimmed a couple of palmetto fronds and propped them up near the fire. He spread Homer's clothes over the palmetto fronds, and they began to steam dry in the heat of the fire. J. J. also cleaned and staked out a few mullet to cook so the boy would have something to eat. Homer now sat naked as a jay-bird before the warm fire with fish enough to fill his stomach.

Suddenly, the night was shattered by the scream of a wild Florida panther. Homer nearly jumped out of his skin! J. J. just listened quietly and sniffed the air testing it with a damp finger.

J. J. reassured Homer. "Calm down son, that panther just smells the fish cooking, and he's at least an hour away to the south. Now, I'm going to go get a few more fish. Then we can head home. You just stay here and keep that fire going till I get back." And J. J. headed off towards the boat.

Homer moved as close to the fire as he could get. Soon, he was warm and full of freshly cooked mullet. At first, every sound drew his attention. But, like most kids, when they are warm, full of good food, and slightly bored, he soon began to drift off into a dream. As he lay there dozing and dreaming, a sharp snap of a broken twig came from the bushes across the clearing. Homer bolted up instantly. He was now wide-awake and scared! There in the shadows, at the edge of the clearing, stood a huge Florida black bear! That bear was big, and, to Homer's mind, he stood a good fifteen feet high. Remember, Homer was only about nine years old.

Homer glanced at the fire and found it had gone completely out. The bear sniffed the air and found the smell of freshly baked fish enticing him closer. Then he spotted Homer sitting there naked as the day he was born. That bear found himself faced with a choice. Now, bears are smart, but they are also slow. He began to glance from boy to fish and from fish to boy as the gears in his mind slowly worked out the problem. The choice was a real dilemma—baked fish or naked boy. You could almost hear the wheels turn in that bear's head as he tried to decide which was the better meal. He again glanced from naked boy to fish to naked boy to fish. It was at that point that the bear seemed to realize there was a considerably larger portion of boy than there was fish. He went down on all fours and headed directly towards the frightened boy. Homer let out a yell, jumped to his feet and headed for the woods. That was his second mistake, the first was letting the fire go out.

Now that bear saw his meal running off, and that engaged his natural hunting instinct. Down on all fours in a flash, after Homer he went. A bear that big would seem cumbersome, but folks, I got to tell you, he was hungry for a good square meal. He chased Homer through the woods at breakneck speed. Homer literally flew up into the branches of the first tree he saw—a young scrub oak. It was here that Homer made his next mistake. What he failed to take into account is that Florida black

bears can climb. That bear was up the tree in a flash, right on Homer's heels. Bears are experienced climbers and instinctively know how sturdy a given tree might be. They also know how to test it before climbing out on a flimsy, thin limb. The bear also knew that if the limb broke, the boy would go with it. So, when that black bear reached the limb on which Homer sat, it stuck out one huge paw and tested the limb. As the bear's enormous weight began to bend the brittle limb, it made a distinct cracking sound. After three or four good solid pushes, the limb broke and down went Homer.

That was when Homer's luck changed for the better—in a way. You see, he landed in the one spot that that bear couldn't or wouldn't go. Unfortunately it was also the one place where Homer had no desire to be. It was one of those look-before-you-leap scenes, come to life. Directly beneath that limb was the largest patch of prickly pear cactus in all of Southern Florida. Homer landed backside down in the middle of that cactus patch. Fortunately, it was his backside only that landed on a single pad of cactus, in a relatively clear spot at the center of that cactus patch.

Meanwhile, that bear shinnied down that oak tree and stood at the edge of the cactus patch. Once again the bear's mind began working on the problem before him. He stared at the naked boy and at the cactus, at the naked boy and at the cactus. Slowly the wheels turned again in the bear's mind. Then he reached out one of his massive paws and almost gently touched the spines of a single cactus pad. The spines stung him just enough to cause him to hesitate for just a moment. As he did, a breeze sprang up and on it was the smell of fresh, baked fish. The bear paused, remembering the clearing and the fish. He sniffed the air tentatively. Then he took a good long smell, licked his lips, and in one swift move headed off towards the baked fish in a dead run.

Homer looked around at the cactus. He was in agony, and tears rushed to his eyes. This was even worse than granny's peach tree switch. The stinging pain was excruciating. His vision blurred. He was convinced, as he looked around the cactus patch, that he would never get out of it alive. You know how kids are when their imagination takes over. He was doomed to become a shriveled up, human pincushion. Thoughts of being trapped in that cactus patch till he starved, or died of thirst came to his overactive imagination. Eventually, his thoughts began to drift, and he began to think of his mama and how he was going home to meet her in heaven. It was about that time that he heard his name being called quietly. His imagination took over, and he just knew that his mama was coming for him. He began to call her

name and sing her favorite hymn "Shall We Gather at the River."

Suddenly, a voice cut through his daydreaming. "Boy, quit fooling around and look up over your head." Relief flooded his pain-filled body. The voice was familiar; it was his Daddy! He looked up, and there was a rope hanging over the branch of a much sturdier tree that was also nearby. He reached up, grabbed the rope, and J. J. pulled him to safety. Homer hugged his Daddy for all he was worth. J. J. tousled Homer's hair and held him close. Then, he squatted down to look Homer in the eye.

He said, "Now, son, I think you learned a lesson tonight. Best not fall asleep when tending the fire. These critters are afraid of a fire but not of an unarmed, naked boy!" He smiled and hugged Homer tight. Then he continued, "But I do think that particular bear is in for a surprise. You see, I left some good size mullet cooking back yonder in the clearing. As I was leaving to come for you, that panther we heard earlier arrived."

No sooner had these words left J. J.'s mouth than the cry of the panther and the roar of an angry bear filled the night. Homer and J. J. headed for the boat. Homer was so sore from the cactus patch that he had to ride home standing up. Homer tells me that he ate Thanksgiving dinner standing up too. He even claims that up until the day he died he still pulled an occasional prickly pear thorn from a place where it shouldn't be. And that's the story of Homer and the Bear.

REFLECTIONS: *Has a wild animal ever scared you when you were out camping or fishing? Did you run, or sit still and quiet? What happened?*

THE SHOEMAKER AND THE KING

A man named John Filareton told this story in 1940 in the Greek community of Tarpon Springs. People whose ancestors came from another place often preserve stories that include ancient cultural elements, such as kings or chiefs. Oftentimes in folktales, the king represents law and order, integrity, and morality. In this case, the king learns a lesson from a shoemaker.

ONCE UPON A TIME, a poor shoemaker earned his living by asking for work from his neighbors. He went house to house each day, gathering old shoes that needed repair. He would take them home, fix them, and deliver them back to his customers. After collecting his pay, he would purchase food and supplies for his family before returning home. Every night after having supper, he would sit with his family, sing, play music, and enjoy himself. The shoemaker was a happy man.

Then one day, the king, who was a very unhappy man, decided to disguise himself and make a tour of the village. He wanted to see what the people in his kingdom were doing. He continued to disguise himself for a few nights, each time walking through the village, checking up on the people who lived there. He passed by the poor shoemaker's home three nights in a row. Each time, he heard singing and music playing. The third night he decided to find out what was going on.

The king knocked on the door, and the shoemaker welcomed him in. Not knowing that the visitor was the king, the shoemaker invited him to sit. The king was treated to food and wine. After some pleasant small talk, the king asked the shoemaker, "Why are you so happy?"

The shoemaker explained that every day after he had finished his work, which was repairing shoes, he would purchase food and supplies for his family. And every night after a good supper, he would sing, play music, and enjoy his family. His being with his family after a good day of work made him happy, and he enjoyed every night.

The king stayed for a little while longer and then left. On his way back to the palace, he became troubled. He saw how the poor shoemaker was a happy man while he, the king, who had everything, was so unhappy.

Being not only an unhappy man, but a mean one, the king decided to make the shoemaker unhappy as well. So, the next morning an announcement was made by the town crier that, by strict orders from the king, no one was permitted to seek work and repair shoes in the streets.

The poor shoemaker, of course, felt very sad, but being a practical man, he said to himself, "What shall I do now to earn our daily bread?" And, as he was walking down the street, a nearby merchant saw the troubled man and felt sorry for him. So the merchant asked the shoemaker to sell some eggs he had on hand. The merchant said they would share the profits, splitting them in half. The shoemaker was glad for the work and successfully sold all the eggs and earned much more that day than the previous days. He again bought food and supplies for his family, had supper, and sang, played music, and enjoyed himself.

The king, wearing his disguise again, took his usual tour about the village. Passing by the shoemaker's home, he heard the same celebrating. When he entered the house, he was welcomed again and treated with kindness. The shoemaker explained that the king of the village had announced that no one was permitted to seek work and repair shoes in the streets. But, he continued, he had earned much more than usual that day by selling eggs. His plan was to continue this new trade to earn money and take care of his family. After a while the king, quite disturbed by what he had heard, returned to his palace.

The next morning the shoemaker went on his way to the merchant's place for more eggs. Before he got there, he heard the town crier say that, by strict orders from the king, no one was permitted to peddle any kind of merchandise in the streets.

The shoemaker was very disappointed, and began wondering, once again, how he was going to support his family. As he walked through the streets, he passed by the tavern where he usually brought wine. After the tavern keeper heard about his troubles, he asked the shoemaker to work for him. Being alone, the tavern keeper explained he could not stay at the tavern all day until closing time. He suggested the shoemaker work the later hours so the owner could have some rest. The poor shoemaker accepted the merchant's kind offer, and worked that day until the later hours, making more money than he had the day before. On his way home, he again bought food and supplies for his family. They had a good dinner, sang and played music, and the shoemaker was happy.

Now the king was rather anxious as he walked the street past the shoemaker's house. When he heard the usual celebrating, he was very angry. But he calmed himself and entered the shoemaker's home. As usual, the disguised king was welcomed and treated with kindness. The shoemaker explained again that, by strict orders of the king, no peddling of any merchandise could take place and that he had gotten work in a local tavern making more money than he had selling eggs or repairing shoes. After a while, the king, quite disturbed by what he had heard, returned to his palace.

This time the king was more determined than ever to make the shoemaker unhappy. The next day he sent two soldiers to the shoemaker's home and told him to appear at the palace.

The shoemaker reported as he was ordered. Not recognizing the king, because he was not in disguise, the shoemaker was told by the ruler that he would become a soldier. The shoemaker obeyed. He was dressed in a uniform and ordered to stay at the entrance of the palace as guard. His job was to snap to attention and, in a formal way he was taught, to display his weapons to everyone who visited him at the palace. The king also gave orders that the shoemaker should stand all day without food, and in the evening he was to leave his gun at the palace. He was not to be paid for his work guarding the palace. When the day ended, the shoemaker was told he could go home but he was to return the next day.

The poor shoemaker, hungry all day, began thinking about what he would do to provide food and supplies for him and his family. When it was time to leave for the day, he left his gun and carried the bayonet with him. Passing by a blacksmith shop, he decided to enter. He asked the blacksmith to cut off the blade of his bayonet and give him its worth in cash. The blacksmith, who was good at making different knives, thought he could easily make a knife and sell it and get his money back with profit. So he bought the bayonet and the shoemaker made more money than he had ever had before for a day's work. On his way home, the shoemaker bought food and supplies for him and his family. They had a good supper, sang and played music, and the shoemaker enjoyed himself. He was a happy man.

The king, disguised as usual, passed by the shoemaker's house and, once again, heard the familiar happy celebrating. Madder than ever before, he had to calm himself before entering the house. The shoemaker welcomed the king and treated him with the usual kindness. The king could see that the shoemaker had fared quite well by his sale of the bayonet at the blacksmith's shop and that he was happier than ever. After a while, the king, more disturbed by what he had heard than ever before, returned to his palace.

In the meanwhile, the shoemaker replaced the bayonet blade with a wooden blade and returned the next morning to his post at the palace. That day one of the criminals was to be executed by having his head cut off. Just as the executioner was getting ready to do his duty, the king ordered the guard (who was, of course, the shoemaker) to cut the prisoner's head off.

"But your majesty," said the shoemaker, "I have never hurt anyone, and I don't wish to cut anyone's head off."

The king replied that these were his orders, and that they must be obeyed.

The shoemaker knew he was in a bad situation. But being the kind of man who knew what to do in difficult situations, he said, "In the name of God and the king, if this prisoner is innocent, may my bayonet turn to wood so his life will be saved. But if he is guilty, may my bayonet remain with its sharp blade as it usually is, so that this man can be executed."

The king immediately saw that the shoemaker had won. He saw that the wooden knife would not cut the prisoner who would be saved and the shoemaker would not have to hurt anyone. Even in this situation, the shoemaker would come out a happy man. The king stopped the execution, and explained to everyone there that the shoemaker was a good man whose ambition in life was to support his family. The king and the town learned a great lesson and the shoemaker was sent home to his family. He lived the rest of his days as a happy man.

REFLECTIONS: *Why do you think the king was unable to make the shoemaker unhappy? Do you think the king became happier himself at the end? Why or why not? What is the message this story teaches?*

THE PREACHER AND THE DUCKS

Almost every adult has a story about something that they did as a child to "get out of a fix." This one comes from Phyllis NeSmith's grandmother. Here, NeSmith tells us the story she heard as a child. Retelling stories told to us by our ancestors helps us remember them, as well as the conditions and context in which they lived. It also helps us associate with them since many of the predicaments they experienced seem familiar to us.

GRANDMA FREEMAN grew up in Nocatee, Florida. All of us grandchildren loved to hear her tell stories about the good old days—back when she was "jest a girl." My favorite was about the time she learned to cook. She always started it the same.

"The summer that I was eleven, Mama got a brand new cook stove. It was shiny black cast iron with lots of chrome trim. It had two warming drawers up top—along beside the chimney—and two big burners, two middle sized burners, and one little burner on the stovetop. The firebox was on the left side. Then came the oven—it even had a thermometer on it, so you could make sure you had the right temperature. And then on the right was the reservoir. That was a big, covered container that you could fill with water, and always have warm water without using the teakettle.

"Well, Mama taught me how to cook on her new stove that summer. Yes sir! I learned how to build up the fire, what kind of wood to use for kindling, what kind to add to keep the temperature just right, which burners were the hottest, how to check that oven. I learned everything about that stove.

"One Saturday, Mama said, 'We've invited the new preacher over for dinner tomorrow. I think I'll leave you home to mind the stove while we're gone to church. You've been doing real good with your cooking.'

"I was *so* proud! I was going to be in charge! I said, 'Yes, Ma'am, what are we going to have?'

"'Well,' Mama said, 'I believe we'll have duck.'

"So she and I went out to the chicken yard and caught us a couple of ducks. Now, Mama killed those ducks. I just wasn't quite up to that, but I helped her clean them. Then we put them out in the spring house to stay cool till the next morning.

Next morning, Mama said, 'Child, you come help me stuff these two ducks, and then check on the fire.' When the ducks were ready, and she had put them in the oven, she said, 'You keep this fire going just like it is. Check on those ducks every so often, and when they're golden brown, take them out of the oven, set them here on the kitchen table, and cover them with a dish towel until we get back from church.'

"'Yes Ma'am,' I said.

"Daddy drove up into the front yard about then in the buggy, and Mama put on her hat, and off they went to church.

"There I was alone! I was in charge! I cleaned up that kitchen—just like Mama would do. After I finished with the dishes, I even threw the rinse water out in Mama's flowerbed—just like she would do. And I kept checking those ducks! When they got nice and brown, I put them on the table—just like I was told—and covered them with a cloth. Oh! They did smell good! I raised that cloth to look at them and thought, I could take just a little nibble to check to see if they were as good as they smelled. So I did. It was delicious, so I took another nibble, and then another, and do you know, I just nibbled those ducks until they looked like they had been in a battle.

"'Oh my!'" I said to myself. 'Mama is going to kill me!'

"Just then the buggy came driving up into the yard. They were here!

"What was I going to do? I covered up those ducks and ran out to the porch. Mama was jut coming up the steps with the new Preacher. 'Howdy,' I said, as polite as I knew how.

"And Mama said, 'This is my daughter, Preacher. You all just go into the parlor while I get the dining room ready.'

"'Yes, Ma'am,' I said and we went into the parlor.

"That preacher started talking. I don't know what he said. All I could think of was the fact that my mama was going to kill me when she saw those ducks. He kept talking and I kept thinking, what can I do?

"I heard Daddy out on the back porch. He was coming up from the barn where he'd taken the horse and buggy to unhitch them. He went into the kitchen and opened one of the cabinet drawers. The preacher was still just talking away.

"Daddy closed that drawer, and went back out to the back porch.

"I knew what he was going to do, and then it came to me—what I could do! I looked at the preacher—still talking. I thought, it's now or never! I began crying—'Boo hoo, boo hoo,' I squalled.

"The preacher stopped in mid-sentence. 'What ever is the matter?'"

"I said, 'Do you hear my Daddy?'

"'Why, yes. Sounds like he's sharpening a knife.'

"You could hear Daddy out on the porch using his whetstone to sharpen his carving knife. He was fixing to carve on those ducks.

"'Boo hoo, boo hoo! That's what he's doing—he's sharpening his knife, and I can't tell you what he's fixing to do with the knife!'

"'What are you talking about, child?' the preacher asked.

"'Well,' I replied, 'My daddy collects preacher's ears, and he's fixing to come in here and cut off your ears. Boo hoo, boo hoo.'

"That preacher jumped up, 'What!' he said and headed for the door. He ran down the steps, and out through the yard, and just kept on going.

"About then Daddy came into the parlor, carrying that knife he'd been sharpening. He looked around and asked, 'Where's that preacher?'

"'Oh Daddy,' I said, 'you're never going to believe what that preacher did.'

"'What are you talking about, child?'

"'Well, Daddy, that preacher went into the kitchen, grabbed those two ducks, stuck them in his pockets, and headed off down the road.'

"'What?' Daddy yelled and ran out onto the porch. Sure enough. There was that preacher running off down the road.

"Daddy, still holding that knife, yelled 'Preacher, you come on back here.'

"That preacher turned around, saw Daddy with that knife, and yelled back, 'Durned if you'll get either one!' and he kept on going.

"We never did see him again, but just about that time, my Mama discovered those ducks in the kitchen. I tell you—I sat down very carefully for the next couple of days."

REFLECTIONS: *Have you ever been tempted to eat something that had just been baked that was made for company? Did you sneak a taste or were you able to resist? Describe one of those times. Were you caught, and, if so, what happened?*

AUNT HAZEL

This tall tale is about Myra Davis's Aunt Hazel, who was a strong and independent pioneer woman. It is a family story, told by Davis, that explains why some things in Florida are the way they are. It also draws attention to how creative and persevering women often had to be in the early years of Florida history—that is, if you believe Aunt Hazel existed. Many of Florida tales highlight male heroes, but most families also have good stories about colorful women relatives. Aunt Hazel is one such spirited character.

ALL MY LIFE I have heard that I take after my Aunt Hazel Hybrid, and that, in itself, makes me feel proud. You see, she was the first liberated woman in Florida, although she never knew it. Aunt Hazel was born in the small town of Bradley, Arkansas. Her family came to Florida when she was only nine years old. During that long, hard trip through four states, she lost her mother to pneumonia. That didn't stop Papa Hybrid. He, along with his seven children, pushed on to Florida. This was the land in which he could fulfill his dream of owning a farm and raising cattle. He had been told that Florida was a place where you could grow fruits and vegetables all year long, and that the weather was sunny, and the air was clean. It was just right for raising children. After traveling several weeks, they settled in a small town named Fort Blount. There Papa Hybrid claimed as his a beautiful piece of land and started farming his vegetables.

For seven years Aunt Hazel, being the oldest girl, helped raise her siblings. When Aunt Hazel wanted to strike out on her own, Papa knew she was strong willed and spirited enough to succeed.

So Papa thought it best to give her his blessing and let her go. He wanted to help his oldest daughter get started so he gave her enough money for a new beginning, a good horse, a flat-bed wagon, and a fresh milk cow. She also took a few chickens, a hound dog for hunting, a cat for chasing mice, and the runt piglet from the sow's litter.

Off she headed. She got as far as West Lake Wales when she spotted a piece of land that was just what she wanted. Here she staked out her homestead claim, and started clearing the land and cutting logs for her cabin. By the time she had finished building her home, four months had passed. She then cleared more land to farm, just as her daddy had taught her to do.

She was never satisfied with growing ordinary fruits and vegetables. No sirree, she always wanted to grow bigger and better strawberries and tomatoes. She would graft one plant to another until she thought it was right, and grow the most beautiful fruits and vegetables you ever saw. She became so famous for her grafting that people came from as far away as Plant City to get her strawberries. Why, to this day, they still call them Hybrid strawberries and Hybrid tomatoes. Even the citrus growers ask for Aunt Hazel to help them with their grafting.

Everyone loved Aunt Hazel. Everyone, that is, except John Tate, who had the personality of a dishrag. Ole John Tate lived just about four miles down the road from Aunt Hazel. From what I was told, he never did an honest day's work in his life. As a matter of fact, all his work was dishonest and done at night. He stole everything that wasn't nailed down. Why, if you passed his place on a Sunday afternoon and smelled chicken and dumplings, you could bet your bottom dollar it was your chicken.

This made Aunt Hazel very nervous. You see, she had become attached to that

little runt of a pig her daddy gave her. She named her pig "Piggy Sue" and raised her inside the house. She even made a highchair for her that had a feeding tray on it so Piggy Sue could sit at the table with her and eat. That little pig would eat so much at times that she made an absolute hog of herself.

Aunt Hazel did some courting once with a man from Lake Wales. His name was Clarence Eugene Bok or Bokum or something like that. I don't know much about him, but I do know he was a jeweler and called Aunt Hazel his princess. So in love with his princess was he that he fashioned and cut a diamond for her. He gave this special cut her pet name—the princess cut. That's what I've been told, but I could be wrong.

Nothing ever became of that courtship except a lot of fine diamond and gold jewelry—which Aunt Hazel wore all the time. Clarence was so heartbroken over loosing his "Jewel of the Ridge" that he built a tower somewhere in Lake Wales. I think they call it the Bok Towers. Clarence lived there until the day he died. At least I think that's the way the story goes.

The only thing Aunt Hazel loved as much as her jewelry was that pig. I was also told that Aunt Hazel became the first farmer to pierce animals' ears for identification. Yep, all of Aunt Hazel's animals got their ears pierced—some of them

doubled pierced. And all of them, except Piggy Sue, got plain gold rings in their ears, but since Piggy Sue was special to Aunt Hazel, and because she was a July baby, she got rubies and gold, which made that pig happier than eating slop.

Aunt Hazel soon learned that, in Florida, hurricanes are a fact of life. She called them Mother Nature's Fury. Well, that's really where this story begins. It was in the early 1900s, and a storm was brewing up to be the biggest ever. The torrential rain and gusty winds were threatening to cause a lot of damage. Aunt Hazel knew what needed to be done. She picked up everything that would blow away. Then she started picking all the ripe, or almost ripe, vegetables and fruit and brought them inside to be canned later. She boarded up the window, pumped water to have inside the house, cleaned out her spare room, and brought all her animals inside. Then she waited out the fury of the storm.

The winds tore the shutters off the windows, the shingles off the roof, and pulled trees up by their roots. I heard that the wind blew so hard that it picked up whole pastures and moved them down the road. For hours Aunt Hazel ran about moving furniture and putting buckets under the leaks from her roof.

Finally the calm came. This is the middle of the storm, which can be pretty quiet. She went out to repair the roof before the rain started again. She let all her animals out so they could get relief. It was still dark and dreary, and before Aunt Hazel had all the shingles back on, the rains started back up and the wind started to howl again. Aunt Hazel gathered all her animals to go back inside. But Piggy Sue was missing. Aunt Hazel called and searched until the winds and rain became so strong that she was forced to go inside. There she made herself some hot coffee, put on dry clothes, and sat by the fire praying Piggy Sue had found shelter.

As soon as the storm was over, she set out to search for Piggy Sue again. As she walked down the road, calling out Piggy Sue's name, tears ran down her cheeks and bubbles came out of her nose. When she came to John Tate's house, John was sitting out on his porch watching his children clean up the mess that the storm had caused. Aunt Hazel ran to the porch to ask him if had seen her pig.

"Most likely it drowned in all that rain," said Tate.

Aunt Hazel would have left it at that had it not been for that ruby earring she saw lying on the ground at the foot of John Tate's porch steps. All the way back home she tried to think of how she could get her pig back before the Tates had pork chops for Sunday dinner.

When evening came, she bridled up the horse and packed a knapsack. In the sack, she put a cat-call which she had made to sound like a Florida black panther. She also packed boot paste that she had made from berries and paraffin, and a strong rope. She rode to John Tate's place and waited in the bushes until nature did its calling, which was around two o'clock in the morning. Sure enough, out came John Tate dressed only in his red flannel underwear with the button-up flap in the back. Tate went into the two-seater outhouse.

When he was inside and comfortable, Aunt Hazel went to work. Dressed in black with the boot polish caked on her face and only her green eyes showing, she crept up to the crack in the outhouse door and let out a panther call as loud as she could. John Tate jumped up so suddenly that he hit his head on the newspaper rack nailed to the side of the wall. Down came all the Sears and Roebuck catalogs. As fast as lightning, Tate grabbed that door and slammed it shut, holding on as tight as he could. Aunt Hazel latched the front door, and put her rope all around the outhouse and tied it securely. Then, she climbed up the tree beside the outhouse. With her long fingernails, she clawed the metal roof and gave out another panther call. Through a hole in the tin roof, Tate could see only one of her big green eyes. Why, you could hear John Tate screaming for ten miles.

Down Hazel came, took her rope, and off she ran to the back of the smokehouse. There in a cage was her beloved Piggy Sue, along with several chickens and rabbits. Aunt Hazel let them all out, and in all the chaos, they scattered everywhere. Then Aunt Hazel ran around to the front of the porch to pick up Piggy Sue's earring.

From inside the house she heard one of Tate's boys yell at his sister. "Katie, bar the door."

Aunt Hazel didn't wait around any longer. She headed for the woods, jumped on her horse, and holding Piggy Sue tight, rode four fast miles home.

The next day, John Tate rode from house to house telling everyone about the killer panther that pinned him in his outhouse and ate all his chickens and pigs. When he saw Aunt Hazel sitting and rocking on her front porch, he stopped to tell her all about his night's adventure. He was still so shook-up that he didn't even notice Piggy Sue in Aunt Hazel's arms as they talked. He told Aunt Hazel that it was the biggest panther he had ever seen and how he came face-to-face and eyeball-to-eyeball with it.

It was shortly after that when Ole John Tate became the first person in Polk County to bring an outhouse inside his home. Why, to this day, to this very day, people are so grateful to him that they still call it the John.

Well, as for my Aunt Hazel, she's passed on now, but her legend still lives on for all of us to enjoy. Her jewelry was passed on to me. As for Miss Piggy Sue, well she's gone now too. But there was a songwriter in the 1950s who was inspired by her and her story. He wrote and recorded a song called "Piggy Sue, I love you, My Piggy Sue." But I really don't see how a song like that would sell! Do you?

REFLECTIONS: *Do you know what grafting is to a farmer? If you don't, who do you think might be able to explain it to you? Is there any truth to what the storyteller says about the Bok Towers? How can you find out? What about that song about Piggy Sue? Have you ever heard it?*

THE CUCARACHITA MARTINEZ

A cucarachita is a lady cockroach. This tale about Cockroach Martinez was collected in Spanish, from the Ybor City, West Tampa area, by Ralph Steele Boggs and published in Spanish in the Southern Folklore Quarterly *in March of 1938. Maria Redmon was the translator. While the Ybor City–West Tampa area is rapidly changing, when Boggs documented this story, Spanish and Cuban people populated the area, originally drawn there by the development of the cigar industry. By 1938, the Depression had hit this region hard, since cigars are a luxury item.*

This story was brought to Florida by the Spanish and still carries a reference to the homeland. Variations of the tale typically focus on an ant and a mouse instead of a cockroach and a mouse. The tale is also well known in Cuba.

ONCE UPON A TIME there was a cucarachita named Martinez, who was sweeping the floor of her house and found a coin. She started to think about what she would do with this coin, and she said to herself: "If I spend it on sweets, I'll eat them, and then they will be all gone, and I'll have nothing. If I spend it on bread, I'll eat it and I'll have nothing."

So she thought some more about what she would do with the money, and after a while she decided she would spend it on flour from Castille. She went to the mill

and bought the flour. She jumped into the flour and reappeared all white covered in the flour. She sat outside at the door of her house for all to see her as they went by.

Soon Mr. Goat went by her house and said: "How beautiful you are, Cucarachita Martinez! Will you marry me?"

And she answered: "Yes, but you must tell me what sound you make at night."

Mr. Goat answered: "Well I say 'bah, bah, bah!'"

"Oh no, you frighten me!" said Cucarachita Martinez.

So the goat went on his way.

A short time later, Mr. Bull passed by her house and said: "How beautiful you are, Cucarachita Martinez! Will you marry me?"

"Yes," she said, "but you must tell me what sound you make at night."

Mr. Bull answered: "Oh, I say 'bu-u-u, bu-u-u!'"

"Oh no, you frighten me!" said Cucarachita Martinez.

So the bull continued on his way.

Soon Mr. Dog went by Cucaracita Martinez's door and said: "How beautiful you are, Cucarachita Martinez! Will you marry me?"

"Yes," she said, "but you must tell me what sound you make at night."

Mr. Dog answered, "Well, I say 'bow-wow, bow-wow.'"

"Oh no, you frighten me!" said Cucarachita Martinez.

So the dog continued on his way.

Later on the Little Mouse Perez passed by and after greeting Cucarachita Martinez said: "How beautiful you are, Cucarachita Martinez! Will you marry me?"

"Yes," she said, "but you must tell me what sound you make at night."

Mr. Mouse answered, "Oh, I say 'squeak, squeak.'"

"Oh, how wonderful!" said Cucarachita Marinez, "I will marry you." And they were married.

One day Cucarachita Martinez was going shopping, so she asked her husband to take care of the food cooking on the stove. She warned him not to look inside the pot because he could fall in.

Once Cuarachita Martinez had left, the mouse decided to take a look inside to see what was cooking. After he looked inside, he could not resist the delicious smell of what was cooking and decided to try some of it. But just as he was ready to try some, he fell into the pot and died.

After awhile Cuarachita Martinez returned home. She knocked on the door—knock, knock! But the Little Mouse Perez did not come to the door. She knocked again—knock, knock! But no one came to the door. Then she became very frightened and worried. She knocked again with all her might—knock, knock! But no one answered.

She then decided to call a carpenter to open her door. The carpenter came with all his tools and tore down the door. When Cucarachita Martinez got to her house, she went running to the kitchen to look for the Little Mouse Perez, but she couldn't find him anywhere.

Then she remembered the pot that she had asked him to watch and thought that he might have fallen in. And so she looked in the pot and found poor Mr. Mouse Perez dead. After crying with sorrow for the Little Mouse Perez, she went outside to the door of her house and sat in a chair and began to sing:

Poor Little Mouse Perez
he fell into the pot
for a taste of food
that he never got.

The End!

REFLECTIONS: *What is the moral to this story? Can you think of other stories that have the same moral? What do you think about Cucarachita Martinez looking beautiful with flour all over her? What might be said about the kind of reaction she got looking like this?*

THE BUNNY RABBIT

Animal fables are told around the world. Fables, such as this one, are animal tales with a message to impart. A fable uses narrative metaphor to teach a lesson. The lesson can be moral, but more often it is about how to make one's way in the world. The truth is a kind of worldly wisdom that easily translates from culture to culture.

Animals in fables take on human traits. In this one, not only can the rabbit talk, but he also lives in a house and has a mother that might sound like any child's mother. This approach to storytelling helps the young child identify with the lesson being taught.

This fable is commonplace and clearly aimed at children. It was told in Spanish in the Ybor City area in the 1930s. Ralph Steele Boggs documented it, and Maria Redmon did the translation.

ONCE UPON A TIME there was a bunny who wouldn't obey his mother. One day his mother said to him: "I have to go out today, and I don't want you to go outside."

In spite of his mother's orders, as soon as his mother left, the bunny went outside. He had decided to explore the forest, so he started running from here to there. "Hippety, hoppety, hippety, hop, hip, hop," were the sounds his paws made as he ran. Finally he was ready to go home, but he couldn't find his way. Soon it was dark, and the poor little bunny didn't know what to do.

All of a sudden he saw a little light in the distance. Little bunny was so happy! He thought that the light was coming from his house, so he walked towards it. But as he got closer to the house, he could see that the house was not his house after all, and he was very sad.

Magically, the door of the house opened, and with a quick hop he was inside. He was so tired that he soon fell asleep on the floor.

Soon after he had fallen asleep, a witch appeared. She was very ugly. Her hair covered part of her horrible face. Her nose looked like an owl's beak, and her eyes looked like a crab's eyes. "Ha! Ha! Ha!" laughed the witch when she saw the pretty little bunny asleep on the floor. The bunny woke up when he heard the laughter.

"What are you doing in my house?" asked the witch.

"Nothing . . . nothing," said the little bunny.

"Well! You will be punished for having dared to come into my house," said the witch. "I would gladly eat you, but today I already have had a great big meal."

Then she touched the little bunny with a wand, and he was changed into a little pig. "Oink, oink, oink" was all he could say now. Poor little bunny! Now he rooted himself in the mud and stomped his hooves about as he explored the forest once again.

This time he found his way home, and when he got home, he knocked on the door. His mother opened the door, but since the poor little pig could only say "oink, oink," she got a stick and chased him away.

The sad and tired little pig went back to the forest. Nearby in the forest there was a hunter, and as soon as he saw the little pig, he caught him and tied a rope around his neck. He took him home and gave him to his wife, saying, "Look, dear, what a fine little pig I have brought for supper."

"Yes, dear," she said, "but you had better take it to the backyard, and cut off its head."

And that is what the hunter did. He tied the little pig to a tree and began to sharpen his axe. The whole time the pig could not stop trembling. The pig was screaming for his mother, but the only words that came out of his mouth were "oink, oink!" When the hunter came over and let the axe fall on the pig's throat and cut off his head, a bunny hopped out.

As bravely as he could, the little bunny ran home without stopping, and all he could hear were his paws going "hippety, hoppety, hippety, hoppety," all the way home.

When he got home, his mother jumped up and down with joy. The little bunny told his mother everything that had happened to him and promised never ever to disobey her again and leave the house when she tells him not to.

REFLECTIONS: *Does this sound like another bunny story you have heard before? What are the differences? Is the moral the same?*

UNCLE LUKE

This is a contemporary family story Dr. Stephen Caldwell Wright tells about his Uncle Luke. Dr. Wright's family has deep roots in the Central Florida area, and he readily tells stories about people, places, and things. This tale is about a memorable character who seems gruff but has his soft spots.

All families have folklore, which includes family stories. We can learn a lot from family stories. This story includes local history, work-related lore, and a keen sense of inventiveness.

UNCLE LUKE WAS ONE of the most colorful characters in the family. He was rivaled only by his brother, an equally proud man called Preacher. Both men, who were strong in physical strength and in their beliefs, had brought all kinds of attention to themselves. They were both known throughout the town as courageous and "sporty," but Luke was thought of as the meaner of the two. Often he had his turn at teaching men and women the cost of crossing him.

But this story is about my Uncle Luke, who spent most of his life, we thought, as a cowboy. He looked at me with cocked eyes and muttered, "Cowboy? What cowboy? They wouldn't even let me near the damn horse!" He went on, "I had a dog and a monkey and a motorcycle. I went to Texas. The dog rode on the seat in front of me, and the monkey rode on the handlebars. Cowboy, my ass!"

I was astonished by what he was saying, but I knew he always told the truth. I just looked at him and let him talk. You had to let Uncle Luke have his say, and he cussed his way through every word. As children we loved it; we loved to see the shock on the faces of the church-going folk, even on our grandmother's light brown face that turned crimson below her deep black eyes.

Uncle Luke was also a skilled, self-taught woodcarver. Whenever he came to our house, he always brought carvings for our grandmother. Sometimes, he would call one of the children over to his knee, and then he would present the lucky "chosen" one with a delicately carved horse or the figure of a man or woman, with triangular mirrors as part of a geometric design.

His eyes would glance away from us, and sometimes we thought we saw the makings of a smile. But because of his temper and the history of his love for physical confrontation with his brother or anyone else, we loved and feared Uncle Luke.

Years after his death, I was sitting with a friend, and we were discussing our families. I had often mentioned Uncle Luke, and on that occasion, I mentioned him again.

My friend, Elena, paused and asked, "Surely, the Uncle Luke you mention can not be the same Luke that we knew?"

I paused and asked, "Do you think so?"

She continued, "Well, he did work on that ranch that my cousins owned. Out near Lake Jessup."

"Then he is the one. Yes. That's my Uncle Luke. He worked out there," I answered.

She responded, "You can't mean it."

I replied, "Oh yes. As a matter of fact, he took me and my brother out there when we were small kids, and we watched him herd the cattle."

My dear friend looked puzzled, even as she beamed with recollected joy and admiration.

Then she continued, "I have got to share this with you. Your Uncle Luke, bless his heart, was the most intriguing person. When we were very little things, we would be taken on hunting trips, but we would walk around the lake while the men hunted. You won't believe this. Your Uncle Luke did the most wonderful thing."

"What did he do?" I asked warily.

"On those cold, cold mornings, when Daddy and his friends were hunting in the woods, we would walk around the lake. Your Uncle Luke was our guide. He took care of us, and the most incredible thing is that on those frosty mornings, Luke would walk us out to the edge of the path that led around the lake. Then Luke would pull from his satchel—hot, baked sweet potatoes. He would give me two and hand two to my sister.

"Take these," he would say in a stern yet calming voice, "Hold these in your hands. Now put them in your pockets."

"As the cold air bit against our little bodies, we would walk around the lake with the warmest hands." She paused and then said, "And that's your Uncle Luke?" She ended with a smile as she shook her head in reflective wonder.

"Yes it is," I chimed and beamed with awe and pride.

To myself, I thought of my Uncle Luke sitting on a bench in his last years at the corner of Sanford Avenue and Third Street, where he deftly carved squares of wood with his scratchy hands and cussed and grumbled out of the delicate spirit that was his true nature.

REFLECTIONS: *Can you tell a family story about one of your uncles or aunts? Is it a family story that gets told often? Who usually tells the family stories in your house? When are they told? How do they make you feel?*

5

Unusual Places, Spaces, and Events

In March of 1998, I attended an event sponsored by the Florida Humanities Council. It was one of their annual Gathering events, that year focusing on Polk County. Musicians Frank and Ann Thomas welcomed the audience, who had come from all over the state, with this bit of folk wisdom: "You always know when you come into Polk County because there's a dead armadillo on the road with a yellow stripe on it." Later, Ann Hyman responded by asking, "Why does the chicken cross the road?" The answer? "To show the armadillo it can be done."[1]

The places where people live and carry on their daily activities have much to do with who they are and who they become. One example of how important the environment can be to one's identity is illustrated by psychologist Roger Barker's 1960s project in which he decided to chronicle the entire days of children, recording as many interactions as he could. After looking over his data, he came to the conclusion that the settings in which the children spend their time are more important to their behavior than their personalities (Gallagher 127). Certain places evoke certain kinds of behaviors and ways of thinking. While some people may assume that folk traditions are more apt to be found in rural areas, many folklorists would disagree. According to Steve Siporin, "the American urban environment may actually intensify the sense of ethnicity and tradition groups bring to the city" (2).

Florida is full of intriguing places that might evoke storytelling activities, both rural and urban. James Goss pointed out that because there have been numerous UFO sightings in Gulf Breeze, near Pensacola, there is much debate amongst believers and nonbelievers, and it has become a popular site to watch for spaceships (96–97). Because serial killer Ted Bundy brutally killed five women at a sorority house at Florida State University in Tallahassee in 1978, fearful tales related to his presence are still told there (9–10). And because hurricanes can be deadly in

Florida, tales of terror about strong winds and rains are always prevalent during hurricane season. Hurricanes can also inspire humorous tales. Glen Simmons, living in the Everglades, explained that after the 1926 storm, for the first time, "we had plenty of chicken to eat. Ours were all dead and scattered out, but good to eat. That's when us young'uns got something besides neck, feet, and legs." He also recalled that that same storm moved their house "half into the glade. We never moved it back, just leveled it up a little" (Simmons and Ogden 12).

Florida's environment can be extreme and harsh in many ways. For example, Glen Simmons spoke about painful fleas he has encountered. "A red-hot fire coal would seem like a piece of ice compared to a gator flea between your toes." They were so troublesome that what he did to avoid them is astonishing. He revealed: "I learned early that the best way to bog the glades was barefooted as the fleas could be got rid of in a hurry. They seem to prefer people wearing loose top boots." However, he noted that going barefoot presented a problem when crawdads were around. "When they start pinching your feet it's hard to stay still, which you have to or else you'll scare a gator that's coming to the top" (65–66). Glen Simmons related another humorous story about camping in the Everglades:

> Since it was a warm night, with only a few mosquitoes and smoke on both sides of me, sleep come easy. I had learned not to sleep on my back because the snoring would wake me up. When I stepped on the rocks around the camp the next morning, my feet hurt so bad that I sat back down on the gator-nest bed. I looked at my feet, and the rats had eaten all the calluses off my feet. They bled very little, but I saw a jillion teeth marks, and I knew I had played hell again. I don't think that my feet ever got over that. . . . There is no feeling in a callus, had there been, I'm sure I would have quit feeding them rats in a hurry. Yes, I put my shoes on. (78)

Other places in Florida evoke other kinds of experiences and other kinds of tales. Anyone who has ever visited Cassadaga and seen a psychic, for example, has a story to tell. Cassadaga is the oldest religious community in the southeastern United States and is the home of a group of Spiritualists (Brotemarkle 106–14). Reverend Jim Watson claims that misconceptions people have about the religion range from "the sublime to the ridiculous" (qtd. in Brotemarkle 106). Teenagers frequent the town on Halloween, thinking they might see a ghost, and local lore includes folk beliefs such as "birds don't fly over Cassadaga."[2]

Festivals are so ubiquitous in Florida, one might be able to find one to go to almost every weekend of the year. In Wausau, for example, people celebrate the opossum in their Funday Festival and especially on the first Saturday in August, which is Possum Day. They have a Possum Concert Choir and a building called the Possum Palace. The focus on opossums certainly encourages tales about this odd little animal (McGregory 103).

Because fishing is such an important activity in Florida, fishing tales can be found everywhere. One Wiregrass region tale that is told when someone comes home without a catch goes like this: "One man says he caught a fish 4 feet long. Other says he caught a lantern that was lit. First protested. Second said that if the first would take a foot off the fish, he'd blow the lantern out" (McGregory 123).

This section of traditional tales includes two Quevedo tales from Ybor City. Quevedo, who was born in Madrid about 1580, is the most well-known legendary folk figure among Florida's Spanish-speaking people. His full name was Francisco Gómez de Quevedo y Villegas. He came from a very influential family, studied with important cultural leaders of the time, and, in his older years, went to live among everyday people. He was a prolific writer who became critical of the ruling class. According to Stetson Kennedy, he has been compared to Seneca as being the catalyst for a cultural renaissance. It is rare to hear Quevedo tales today, but they were popular in the 1930s in both Ybor City and Key West (Kennedy 125–26; Bucuvalas, Bulger, and Kennedy 186–87).

Several African American tales told here survive from earlier times. "Diddy-Wah-Diddy" probably comes out of the experience of poverty where one dreams about unlimited food. According to information collected during the WPA years, there were constant efforts by preachers to keep the minds of slaves on thoughts of a hereafter (McDonogh 28).

In "Big John Gives Old Master a Sign," the slave outsmarts the master. These plentiful tales about Big John are thought to come from African trickster tales, where the trickster was played by the rabbit. The rabbit tales, known most commonly as Brer Rabbit tales, and Big John tales contain many similar characteristics (Joyner 147–49). Daddy Mention tales are probably somewhat related, though Daddy Mention seems to have been a real character. As another incarnation of Big John, Daddy Mention is also looking to escape, not from slavery but from his frequent prison sentences. According to the WPA *Negro Guide*, Daddy Mention represents wish fulfillment. "The wily Big John compensated for the helplessness of the slave in the hands of the master, and Daddy Mention does the same for the convict in the prison camp" (McDonogh xx).

Conditions in prisons during Daddy Mention's time, after the emancipation, were best at Raiford, while conditions in the city and county jails varied. The WPA materials state that Daddy Mention certainly existed because so many people claimed to have known him and many did time with him. Because his tales were so prevalent, the WPA writers note that he must have been continuously incarcerated in places all over the state. But former prisoners "will insist that he was in the Bartow jail on a 90-day sentence, 'straight up' when they were doing 60. Then another will contradict and say it must have been some other time, because that was the period Daddy was in Marion County 'making a bit in the road gang'" (qtd. McDonogh 75). WPA writers claim, quite rightly, that Daddy Mention tales have all the characteristics of the John Henry stories (McDonogh 17–18 and 24–25).

The Daddy Mention tale passed along here takes place in Polk County, the same place where the armadillos are found in the road with yellow stripes on them. Daddy Mention reportedly worked in road camps while in the county jail. One of the songs he might have sung, with a grunt on the end of each line that marks the swing of a axe or other tool, goes like this:

> *Little corn, un huh,*
> *Yaller girl, uh huh,*
> *Little fight, uh huh,*
> *Lotta time, uh huh*
> (McDonogh 54)

Many of the stories in this section have origins that are decades or even a century or more old. As they are repeatedly told, the stories change and adapt to new locations. It is, therefore, often difficult to tell where they began.

MY FIRST JOB

Chuck Larkin, a teller of tall tales, adapts this folktale to meet his own style of relaying a story. Versions of this tale are told throughout the United States. Each one is personalized somehow and is made to fit the local landscape. This tale can be enjoyed not only for its humor but also because of the kind of rhythm that is created when it is read. Whereas most tall tales are short, this one is rather lengthy.

These kinds of stories are often told in an informal tall-tale-telling context. For example, a group of people can be sitting around a campfire or in any regular gathering place and one person (most often a man since tall tellers are generally male) tells a "whopper" and another tries to outdo him with his own experiences. These are usually friendly competitions where exaggeration builds. Larkin is known as a master of tall tales.

WELL, FOLKS, I'm going to tell you about my first job. I was living in Saint Petersburg, Florida, back when the city was smaller, and we had several farms. Ours was out in the northeast near Gandy Bridge. I think I was still nine years old when Mr. Culliton, a neighbor, hired me as his beeboy. Now I know that beeboying may be an unfamiliar occupation to you, so I'll tell you something about it.

I would go over to his farm in the morning and get his honeybees out of their hives. I would then herd them out into the clover pasture. All the while, I'd walk around singing beeboy songs to the bees.

A beeboy song is a lot like a cowboy song. You see, not all the songs that Hollywood put in the movies are really cowboy songs. Some of those songs were originally for honeybees. Beeboy songs are like the songs the cowboys used to sing out on the range to the cows. Most cowboys learned these songs from the beeboys who brought the tunes over from the old country.

When I started work, Mr. Jim Culliton gave me an old rusty rifle with one bullet. I still remember his words. He said, "Chuck, don't let any bears bother my honey bees. Your job is to keep the honeybees happy while they gather nectar. And you must protect them from bears. Don't let any bears get away if you see one bothering my bees!"

It was a good job, until, well, let's say I never will forget the day things got difficult. It was about three weeks after I started working. I was on the far side of the field from the woods when two black bears broke from the woods and grabbed one of the little honeybees that had strayed too close to the tree line. Each grabbed one wing and turned to run back into the woods. You see, bears like the nectar the bees carry on their wings and bodies.

I tore across the pasture with only that old rusty rifle and one bullet. I was screaming like a wolverine. "You bears, turn that honeybee loose!" When you are young, you do silly things like that. The bears entered the woods and ran through the palmetto bushes toward a small creek. I couldn't have been more than thirty yards behind them. When the bears reached the creek, they suddenly turned my little honeybee loose. I was relieved for a moment until I realized that both bears had turned around and were coming toward me. Now I had one bear on my left and one on my right, charging at me. Believe me, that kind of experience can flat out wake you up! There I stood with my rusty rifle and one bullet trying to make a decision. Today that would be easy. I would just appoint a committee.

I turned toward the bear on my left and made that direct eye contact that the books say will slow a wild animal down. I learned that day that people who write books hardly ever go in the woods. They do not know what they are talking about because that bear never slowed down. I watched the bear on my right coming in at me with my peripheral vision. He was closer than I thought, because suddenly he was next to me. Not knowing what else to do, I rammed my hand right down his throat! You might say that surprised the bear. However, he still was coming up my arm. So I grabbed his tongue, pulled and snapped at him until I had turned him inside out.

He was still moving, but now his momentum was carrying him away from me. And that really surprised me! Let me tell you one thing I learned that day. When you turn a bear inside out you think you are pretty hot stuff. At that moment I believed I could do anything!

Now I had to think about that second bear. I still had that rusty rifle and one bullet, so I turned toward him. I was mean, cold-eyed, snorting and ready. So then, after the bear saw what I had done to his buddy he turned around and skedaddled across the creek. Even though I was no longer in danger, I knew I had to follow him. Mr. Culliton had said that my job depended on not letting any bears get away that had bothered his honeybees. So I turned toward the creek.

I did not want to get my feet wet, so I decided to use stepping stones to cross the creek. When I was almost across I suddenly saw a fox break from the bushes on my left. He started to attack me. But I am not scared of any fox, and this fox was no exception. On the other hand, if they get at you they can tear your britches off your legs. So I thought I'll just shoot this one bullet in the fox's direction and scare him off.

I really didn't want to kill this fox, because I do not like to hunt, and that's because I do not like to have to work to carry game out of the woods. I already had a bear to field dress and carry across the fields to Jim Culliton's house, and I figured that was plenty of work already. You may not know this, but bears do not live long turned inside out. So thinking I would only scare the fox, I started to bring my rifle barrel around toward the fox when here comes the fox's mate attacking me from the right. If two foxes get you not only can they tear up your britches, but they can eat up your shoes too. OK, I thought, I'll shoot between the two of them.

All of a sudden I saw a shadow, and I looked up. Flying over my left shoulder in a straight line were nine humongous Canada geese. They were flying so low I knew I could shoot one if I wanted to. And they do taste good. If they are cooked right, they taste like chicken.

Then I noticed a second shadow from overhead, and when I looked over my right shoulder I saw nine mallard ducks. Oh yes, and if they're cooked right they taste good too, just like chicken. I was considering shooting one when I noticed the two foxes were getting mighty close. I turned and fired the bullet from that rusty rifle down between the two of them.

Things sure got confusing after that. The best I could figure out later was that the bullet hit a sharp rock and split in half. The left half of the bullet passed through and killed the fox on the left. It then hit a rock and ricocheted through a large bush. On the other side of the bush, a nine-point buck deer jumped up and fell down dead with half a bullet in his head. I thought, "wow, this is my lucky day!" I did not even know the buck deer was there. Venison, you know, when cooked right, tastes just like chicken.

The right half of the bullet took out the fox on the right, passing right through him. Then that half bullet skipped off a palm tree stump, went through and split a branch of a scrub oak tree over about thirty yards. When the half bullet passed through the branch and split it open, the branch—snap—popped back closed. What was unusual, there happened to be nine wild turkeys roosting on the branch. When it opened and snapped back closed it pinched and caught their toes. There they were flapping their wings and going gobble, gobble, gobble. I thought, this is my lucky day! You know, no matter how you cook turkey, it tastes like turkey.

But wait, there's more. Let me tell you what happened next.

That same half bullet then hit a sharp-edged rock, which then busted up into hundreds of sharp shards of rock. The shards rose into the oak tree overhead, killed, skinned, and field dressed nine squirrels. They came down like huge raindrops, plop, plopity, plop. Yes, you guessed it. When squirrels are cooked right, they taste just like chicken.

You remember I mentioned that I had that old rusty rifle with me! When I shot that bullet, the gun blew up, bawoom! The iron rifle barrel rose up into the air majestically and skewered all nine of the Canada geese. At the same time, the rifle's wooden shoulder stock rose, walloped, battered and killed all nine of the mallard ducks. The force of the explosion blew me back into the water. I landed on top of a school of trout fish and three gar fish. The fish got jammed up in my pockets, in my pants, and under my shirt. A button popped off my shirt, into the air with such velocity, it killed a pheasant flying over.

Now here is the part nobody believes! The pheasant fell down on and killed a rabbit. Yep, both pheasant and rabbit, when cooked right, taste just like chicken.

I looked around at all that carnage. I told you that I do not even like to hunt. But I thought to myself, that, yes, this is my lucky day. But I surely do not want to carry all of that game out of the woods, through the clover pasture, to Mr. Culliton's house.

I took my baby jackknife, which Santa Claus had given me when I was three years old and field dressed the bear and the buck deer. When I got over to the deer— you may not believe this—but I'd walk on my lips before I'd tell a lie. I also discovered a nine-foot diamondback rattlesnake wrapped around a seven-foot alligator. One of the deer's antlers had pierced the snake in the head, passed through and killed him and the gator. That snake had eighteen rattles on its tail. I still have a belt and wallet made from that snake's skin and a backpack made from the gator's hide. That's the truth! I'd eat fried chicken before I'd lie about that. And, yes, rattlesnake meat is good too, when cooked right along with gator tail, it all tastes just like chicken.

With my knife, I cut the deer hide into finger-width strips that I tied end to end. This gave me a deerskin rawhide rope about thirty-six feet long. Next, I rolled up my deerskin rope and soaked it in the creek with a big rock on it so it wouldn't float away. Next, I walked, and cut some long tough stems from a bunch of palmetto bushes, each about nine feet long. I made these into poles that I tied side by side with string I made from the fox skins and squirrel skins. I curved and bent the poles like a boat/raft/sledge and covered the bottom with mud and set it half in the water. This gave me a boat-like ground sledge that looked like a snow sled without runners that could also float. I loaded the bear meat, deer meat, rattlesnake, and alligator meat and hides as well as nine Canada geese, nine mallard ducks, nine squirrels, two foxes, the pheasant, the rabbit, and eighteen trout fish. I threw the gar fish back in the creek. I can tell you I could hardly wait to get the fish out from under my clothes. They tickled something awful. I cut the rack of antlers off the buck deer and tied them tight to the front bow of my sledge boat. On a bottom point of the antlers, I tied the eighteen rattles of the snake. Last I cut off the branch that had the toes of the nine wild turkeys pinched and tied that branch tight to the top of the rack of antlers.

I fetched my wet deerskin rawhide rope out of the water. Then I tied one end of

the rope to the front of my sledge boat. With the other end over my shoulder, I waded in and stretched that wet deerskin rawhide rope out along the creek through the woods, just like a giant rubber band. I pulled it up the little bank and through the clover pasture, about twenty yards past Mr. Culliton's front door. Last, I tied the rope to one of his great oak trees.

I then went back and found my little honeybee. She was happy to get back to the clover pasture. I sang a few beeboy songs until all the honeybees settled down. When they seemed pretty calm, I herded the honeybees back to their hives and put them up for the night. Finally, I went to Mr. Culliton's house and knocked on the door. He came out, and I told Mr. Jim Culliton the same story I just finished telling you. At the end of my tale, I said, "Yes sir, Mr. Culliton, best I could figure I have caught for you all told about sixty-two fish, foul, and beasts."

Mr. Culliton looked at me. "Chuck," he said, "I do not believe you. Do you have any evidence?"

Quick as I could, I replied, "Yes sir, here it comes now."

I had figured that the afternoon sun would have been up over the trees. All after-

noon the sun was drying out the wet, stretched, deerskin rawhide rope. The rope would have been shrinking and pulling that boat/raft/sledge off the bank along the creek through the woods, up and through the clover pasture and the gate to Mr. Culliton's front door.

Now I know there are some skeptics. Somebody always wants to know how a boat/raft/sledge can be pulled up over rough, bumpy terrain. Well, I had that planned. Whenever the raft sledge hit a rock or stump, the rattles would shake and scare the begeebers out of the wild turkeys who were still very much alive. They would beat their wings and lift the sledge over the obstacle.

The raft sledge with all the fish, foul and beasts pulled up by the front door and stopped. "Aren't I lucky?" I said. "This was my lucky day. There is enough meat, after it is smoked—well it ought to last you two years."

Mr. Culliton thought it over for a minute. Then he wanted to know where the second bear was. I told him that after the gun blew up, the second bear got away.

He didn't seem too happy about this part of the story. So he said, "Chuck, today is not your lucky day. I told you not to let any bear get away that was bothering my honeybees. No, this is your unlucky day." Then he shook his head and said, "You're fired."

That is the story of my first job. What is strange, though, is that about a week later Mr. Culliton came over to the house and asked me to come back to work for him. It seems that I had killed the second bear after all. Mr. Culliton explained, "It was the half bullet that split and passed through the tree limb that caught the wild turkeys. That split bullet had killed the bear over about another nine yards in the bushes, so you got sixty-three varmints all told. I'd like to hire you back."

But I told him no, I'd only work where I could have some job security. Later on, though, he did give me two bearskin rugs along with the snakeskin belt and gator hide backpack after he had cured the hides.

And that's a true story.

REFLECTIONS: *What kind of person do you think this storyteller is? If he can tell a story this good, what do you think he does for a living? Can you tell a tall tale about your first job?*

THE MAN AND THE BEANSTALK

As a version of "Jack and the Beanstalk," this tale will seem very familiar. It is a story that has been told all over Britain and the United States. Walt Disney created a humorous animated version of the story, author Toni Cade Bambara wrote a version of it that focuses on race relations, and James Finn Garner's Politically Correct Bedtime Stories *tells the story with vegetarians and a moral about judging others. All versions include many common motifs such as a giant plant that leads into the skies and a hero who must negotiate new territory.*

Whereas the "Jack" version featured a young boy, this rendition is about a grown man. It was documented in the early twentieth century in Florida. Notice how it begins. Like many legends, someone always swears it happened to someone once or twice removed from the teller. It is not clear where Marsh Harbor is. Perhaps this is a local name for a swampy place in Florida.

A FRIEND, who heard it from someone from Marsh Harbor, told this story to me. It happened to him.

He was out walking one day, just walking along leisurely-like across the island where he lived, when he came upon a huge beanstalk like the one Jack of "Jack and the Beanstalk" used. Being curious, he looked it over and tried to see the top of it, but when he looked up, it was so high it disappeared in the clouds, and he couldn't see the top.

After a while, he got more and more curious and wanted to see how far up it went. So he started climbing. The further he climbed, the further he wanted to go. He kept climbing but it seemed like a long time before he reached the top. When the beanstalk came to an end, it was all withered and dried. He discovered that he could crawl out on solid ground, so he crawled off the beanstalk and sat down to rest.

After he had been sitting there for a spell, he saw some women in the distance. He reckoned he would get up and go see who they were and what they were doing.

So he walked over and told them how he got there and who he was. The women then informed him that he was in the first heaven and that they lived there. They said they made garments for all the other folks in heaven. As they talked, they were cutting out material and sewing.

Finally, after a visit, the man claimed he got scared up there, and he reckoned he had better get himself back to where he came from. So he went back to the edge of heaven, to the place where he had come in. But when he got there, he found that the beanstalk had withered and fallen down. He was stranded.

He went back and told the women all his troubles. They were kind women and offered to help him. So they took some of their fabric and tore it up. From the pieces, they braided him a rope so that he could be lowered back to the earth.

The man bid the kind women good-bye after thanking them for their trouble. He went over the side of heaven and began his journey down the braided rope. He lowered himself to thirty feet above the ground. Here the braided rope ended. It wasn't long enough.

He didn't know what to do. He dangled there for a time trying to think what he should do. He couldn't figure out if he wanted to drop head first or feet first. He decided he didn't want to drop feet first, because he was afraid that his feet would be shoved up into him, and he was afraid to go head first because he'd bash his head in. At last he decided that it would be better for him to go head first and he did.

The man landed in the sand, plumb up to his waist. He wiggled and wiggled, trying to get himself loose, but it didn't do any good. He couldn't budge. He figured he was going to have to do something drastic, so after a bit, he walked to a nearby farm and got himself a hoe, came back, and dug himself out.

REFLECTIONS: *How is this story like the "Jack and the Beanstalk" story you know? How is it different? Can you make up a different ending to this story? Would your ending be as silly or more serious?*

DIDDY-WAH-DIDDY

Diddy-Wah-Diddy is the best known of the mythical places from African American folktales. This story was collected in the 1930s. What is described here could also be called "the promised land" or "the land of milk and honey." Versions of this story can be found in many religious texts, including Christian, Buddhist, and Islamic ones.

DIDDY-WAH-DIDDY is a wonderful place to go. Its geography is that it is "way off somewhere." It is reached by a road that curves so much that a mule pulling a wagon-load of feed can eat off the back of the wagon as he goes. It is a place of no-work and no-worry for people and beasts. It is a very restful place where even the curbstones are good sitting-chairs.

The food is even already cooked. If travelers get hungry, all they need to do is sit down on the curbstone and wait. Soon they will hear something hollering, "Eat me! Eat me! Eat me!" and a big baked chicken will come along with a knife and fork stuck in it. You can eat all you want. By the time you feel full of chicken, a big deep sweet potato pie will push and shove to get in front of you. A knife and fork will be stuck up in the middle so you can cut a piece off and eat to your heart's delight. Nobody can ever eat it all up. No matter how much you eat, it just grows that much faster.

They say, "Everyone would live in Diddy-Wah-Diddy if it wasn't so hard to find and so hard to get to even after you know the way." Everything is on a large scale there. Even the dogs can stand flat-footed and lick crumbs off heaven's tables.

The biggest man there is known as Moon-Regulator because he reaches up and starts and stops it at his convenience. That is why there are some dark nights when the moon does not shine at all. He did not feel like putting it out into the sky that night.

Most folks believe this place exists. It sure is good to think about, anyway.

REFLECTIONS: *Why do you think it was so important to African Americans to tell this story in the early twentieth century? Do you think it is just as important for them*

to tell this story today? Why or why not? Who else might want to tell tales about places where there is an unlimited amount of food? Why? Do you know another story about a far-away wonderful place that sounds similar? Can you tell it?

OLD FROSTYSIDES

This story takes place around Fort Meade, one of Florida's main cattle ranching areas. Florida historian Dana Ste. Claire reports that the event depicted here happened to Captain Asbury Hendry, who rode his herds through the Fort Meade area in 1870. However, this version of the story, taken from the Works Progress Administration papers, suggests that it happened to one of the cowmen who worked for Hendry. In any event, Hendry was a well-known Cracker cattle king who purchased thirty thousand acres of land in Hendry County, which was named after him.

Florida's early White settlers had a difficult life. The Cracker cowboy's life was especially rigorous in the early days. Often away from their families, they stayed overnight in camps. At night, they often told stories. The legend of Old Frostysides is still told today.

AT THE END of a long day, the weary cowboys who worked for Captain Francis Asbury Hendry, one of Florida's pioneer cattle kings, headed toward the nearby camp. Their exhausted ponies were quickly unsaddled and turned loose to roll and wallow upon the green sod and refresh themselves. Very soon the welcome announcement that supper is ready is heard from the cook, and the whole party, with appetite whetted down to a keen edge, gather around a bountiful meal. During the day the cook has killed a fat turkey or deer, and its sweet taste renders the meal a luxury which kings might envy.

After supper the cowboys tell of their day's adventures. One tells of an encounter with a wolf, chasing it across a long stretch of prairie and at last killing it with his pistol or heavy stirrup. Another veteran herder mentions a wild and vicious bull that wouldn't behave.

"What became of him?" asks the boss.

"Well," said the old herder, "I frightened him with what bullets I had, but that lead didn't prove to bother him much, and he kept a-going the way I last saw him. He's probably now somewhere in the middle of the Everglades, I reckon. I had such a time of it today, I don't ever want to repeat it."

About then, one of the old cowboys enters the room, having missed dinner. After getting something to eat, he sat down to tell about his day's adventure.

"You boys remember that old cradle-headed steer that gave us the slip last year? We called him Old Frostysides. Well, I had it out with him today, and he just about did me in. I came up to him—or rather he came up to me—and we appeared mighty glad to see each other for a minute. It was right after dinner-time when I ran that small group of cattle around behind Tiger Bay."

The other cowboys said they missed him at dinner and were just about to go looking for him when he turned up.

"I wish you had come, and brought some artillery with you," replied the old herder. "Just as I was a-turning the point of the bayhead, old Frosty came out of that there swamp like a tornado with a great load of vines around his horns. I believe the old cuss must have been mad when he came out. I spurred back my pony Jack and squared myself before him. I gave Old Frosty a few smacks with my whip, trying to get him into the herd, but he came for me full tilt. Back of me was a pile of sawgrass, so boggy it would bog down a saddle-blanket. There was no way to run except into the bog-hole.

"In the middle of this here tussle that saddle-girth of mine broke, and me and Jack parted quicker than lightning. The mud was soft, but bless your life, fellers, Jack just left me and Old Frosty to settle the whole matter between us. The very first thing I saw when I tried to rise up out of the mud was Old Frosty's eyes looking green at me, his tongue out, with ropes of slobber streaming from his mouth and nostrils. He was all set to run through me. All this time my hat had stuck to my head like a leech. How I did it or how I came to think about it, I don't know. But I snatched that hat off my head and swung it at Old Frosty. The point of one of his horns stuck right through the crown and it rested right over Old Frosty's eyes so he couldn't see a thing! This allowed me to make my get-away."

After taking a moment, the old cowboy declared, "I guess my hat's still there, and I hope it rots there."

"Well I swear!" said one of the boys. "We noticed you came in bare-headed, but thought you had hung your hat on your saddle-horn to air your temples a little."

The old herder thought a moment and replied, "It's hanging on a horn all right, but not my saddle horn."

The old man's story ends with the roar of stampeding cattle and the crash of the cow-pen rails.

"Every man to his horse!" cries the boss. "Five of you follow me, and the rest keep up the rear and fix the pens! They're smashed to smithereens!"

No less than a hundred feet of the heavy log rails were knocked flat on the ground, and the cattle poured through and out into the timber. In a short time the boss and his party caught up with the herd of the fleeing cattle, and by riding just ahead of them to an open place, they led them into a circle and they gradually quieted. Some of the cattle were killed outright by the stampede, while others were badly crippled and bruised.

The old cowman who had told the last story swore that Old Frostysides must have come up and caused the stampede. And sure enough, the next morning Old Frosty, hatless now, was standing in the pen with the herd.

REFLECTIONS: *Do you and your family tell stories at the dinner table about what happened during the day? Can you remember telling or hearing an adventure story that challenged you or a family member somehow? Can you repeat that story now?*

RAISING POPCORN

This is another tall tale, or "whopper," told by fiddler/storyteller Richard Seaman at the 1992 Florida Folk Festival in White Springs. The festival takes place on Memorial Day weekend, the beginning of the summer in Florida. It makes sense that Seaman might want to tell a story about how hot it can get. This tall tale, like all good tall tales, stretches the possibility of truthfulness to extremes.

I HAD A FARM, and I raised popcorn down there. Popcorn was my chief crop. And it was awful hot down there in the summertime when the corn was ripe, so I had to take my popcorn to town in a two-horse wagon pulled by two big Kentucky mules. And I would have to carry my popcorn to town at night, because the sun was so hot in the daytime I was afraid the popcorn would blow up.

Well, one day I got a little tight from drinking too much. You know I didn't get a right start in the morning, and I left too late. Well the sun came up and caught me on the way to town, and I had a hangover. And the mules were walking along, and I wasn't much giving a darn what happened. And right around midday, the sun was so hot that the whole wagonload of popcorn just blew up. It blew up right there in the middle of the road.

Well, to top it all off, those two mules turned around and saw it. And they thought it was snow, and both of them froze to death right there.

If that weren't the truth, I wouldn't have told it to you.

REFLECTIONS: *Why do you think the storyteller ended the story by proclaiming he was telling the truth? What kind of man do you imagine Richard Seaman, the storyteller, is? Can you create a tall tale from an experience that happened to you?*

BIG JOHN GIVES OLD MASTER A SIGN

This is an African American story, collected in Florida in the late 1930s. It dates from the time of slavery. Slaves used to tell many stories about how they outsmarted their masters. These tales functioned to keep them hopeful in a world that seemed hopeless. Often, the wise slave who was able to outwit his master was named Big John. Telling tales like this one was, in a way, an act of defiance, as John is able to reverse the circumstances of who is in control.

Tales about Big John told in the days of slavery were enhanced by the response of the audience. In this manner, these tales were communal activities.

OLD MASTER AND OLD MISS had no sooner gotten on the train than Big John sent word to all the other slaves on all the plantations around that Old Master and Old Miss had gone to Philadelphia and won't be back for three weeks. Big John had been left in charge of everything. "Come over to the Big House," he invited everyone. "We'll have a great time."

While the invitation was being passed around, Big John told some of his friends to kill some of Old Master's hogs so they could feast on them.

That night Big John put together a fine table full of lots of food. Everyone who could get a hold of White folks' clothes had them on that night. Big John opened up the entire house and took Old Master's big rocking chair and put it on top of Old Master's bed. Then he climbed up and sat down on it to call out the dance steps. He was sitting in his high seat with a box of Old Master's cigars under his arm and one in his mouth when he noticed a couple of poor White folks coming into the house.

"Take them poor folks out of here," he instructed. "Take them back to the kitchen and don't allow them up front again. We don't want anything out here but quality."

Big John didn't know that these same White folks were Old Master and Old Miss dressed up in rags with dirt on their faces. They had slipped back to see how he would behave while they were gone. Of course, they were not happy. They washed the dirt off their faces and came back up front were Big John was sitting.

"John," said Old Master. "After I trusted you with my place, you went and smoked up all my fine cigars and killed all my hogs and let all those slaves in my house to act like they were crazy. Now I'm going to take you out to the persimmon tree and hang you. You deserve to be hung, and that's what I'm going to do."

While Old Master was gone to get the rope, Big John called his friend Ike to one side and said, "Ike, Old Master is going to take me out and hang me on the persimmon tree. Now I want you to hurry out to that tree and climb up into it. Take a box of matches with you, and every time you hear me ask God for a sign, you strike a match."

After a while, Old Master comes back with the rope, and he leads Big John out to the tree. He ties a noose in the rope and puts it around Big John's neck. He throws the other end over a limb.

"I've got just one favor to ask of you," said Big John. "Let me pray before I die."

"All right," said Old Master, "but hurry up and get it over with, 'cause I've never been so anxious to hang anyone in my life."

So Big John kneels down under the tree and prays, "Oh Lord, if you mean for Master not to hang me, give me a sign."

When he said that, Ike struck a match, and Old Master saw it and began to shake. Big John kept on praying. "Oh Lord, if you mean to strike Old Master dead if he hangs me, give me a sign." Ike struck another match, and Old Master said, "Never mind, John. You've prayed enough. The hanging's off."

But Big John kept on praying. "Oh Lord, if you mean to put Old Master and all of his family to death tonight, give me a sign." This time Ike struck a whole handful of matches, and Old Master lit out from there as fast as he could run.

And that's how the slaves got free. Big John scared Old Master so bad that he ended slavery right then and there.

REFLECTIONS: *Is this a true story about how the slaves got their freedom? Why do you think it was important for slaves to tell stories like this? Do you know any Brer Rabbit stories? How is this story similar to a Brer Rabbit story?*

QUEVEDO ON FRENCH SOIL

Francisco de Quevedo was a Spanish writer who lived from 1580 to 1645. An educated man, he served in diplomatic missions in Italy and was later appointed secretary to King Phillip IV. However, from 1639 to 1643, he was under house arrest, suspected of writing a political satire about the king.

These Spanish tales about Quevedo's antics traveled with immigrants to Ybor City where, in March of 1938, Ralph Steele Boggs documented this story. Maria Redmon translated it from Spanish.

ONCE UPON A TIME the king of Spain was very angry at Quevedo; so much so that he ordered him to leave Spain and her territories and never again put foot on Spanish land. Immediately Quevedo went to the border that separates Spain and France, and, after filling a cart with French soil, he returned to Madrid, Spain. He

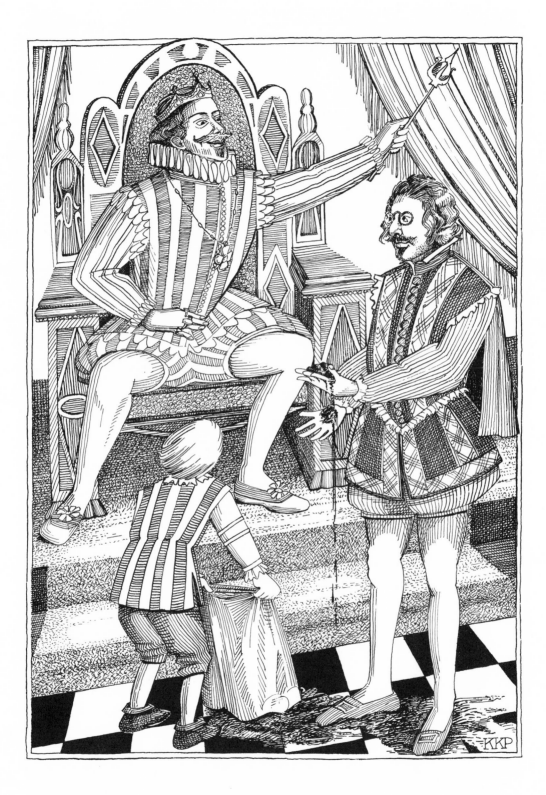

placed the French soil under his feet and stood proudly. When the king saw him, the ruler said: "Quevedo, didn't I tell you never to put your foot on Spanish soil again?"

"Of course you did," answered Quevedo, "I'm on French soil now."

This answered pleased and satisfied the king so much that he pardoned Quevedo.

REFLECTIONS: *If you were king would Quevedo's actions have pleased you? What was it about Quevedo's answer that might have pleased the king?*

QUEVEDO CHOOSES TO DIE OF OLD AGE

When immigrants came to Florida, it was important for them to retain many of the cultural attributes of their home country. The Spanish in Ybor City enjoyed telling stories about Francisco de Quevedo, a talented writer from Spain who lived from 1580 to 1645. His major works include The Life and Adventures of Buscon *(1626; translated in 1657) and* Visions *(1627; translated in 1640).*

This story was collected by Ralph Steele Boggs in the late 1930s and was recently translated by Maria Redmon.

ONCE UPON A TIME the king ordered that Quevedo be put to death. Accordingly, Quevedo was imprisoned, but when the time for the execution arrived, he asked the king if he could choose the way he was to die. The king said that since he was going to die one way or another, he would grant him his last wish. Quevedo immediately answered: "I want to die of old age."

Since the king had given his word, he ordered that Quevedo be freed immediately.

REFLECTIONS: *Describe Quevedo as a man. What would spending an evening with him be like? Would it be enjoyable?*

THE TINY LITTLE CHICKEN

Cumulative stories have repeated elements in them. This form of storytelling is repeated around the world. These types of narratives or songs are fun to learn and repeat because of their patterned rhythms.

Collected by Ralph Steele Boggs in the Ybor City area in the 1930s, "The Tiny Little Chicken" was translated by Maria Redmon.

ONCE UPON A TIME there was a tiny little woman who lived in a tiny little house. In her tiny little house, she had tiny little furniture. In her tiny little garden she had a tiny little chicken. One day the tiny little chicken laid a tiny little egg. The tiny little woman took the tiny little egg and made a tiny little omelet and put it in her tiny little refrigerator to cool. Outside the tiny little house, a tiny little thief saw the tiny little woman put the tiny little omelet in the tiny little refrigerator. When the tiny little woman lay down to take a tiny little nap in her tiny little bed, the tiny little thief came into her tiny little house and opened her tiny little refrigerator and ate her tiny little omelet and took her tiny little chicken who laid the tiny little eggs.

This tale is finished and yours has just begun.

REFLECTIONS: *Why do you think the storytelling ended the tale with "This tale is finished and yours has just begun"? How does the repetition of words enhance the tale? Why do you think the storyteller made everything tiny?*

THE FIG TREE

This tale, from the Ybor City area, was documented in Spanish by Ralph Steel Boggs in the 1930s, and recently translated by Maria Redmon.

Versions of this tale are found around the world. One adaptation has the step-daughter's hair growing as wheat before she is dug up alive.

Stepmothers, around the world, are often depicted as wicked. In most all these tales, at the end, the stepmother is banished or destroyed, indicating that good triumphs over evil. The stepdaughter, who is usually beautiful, is generally victorious in the end.

Folklore is full of stories about people who turn into trees. Some people who ana-lyze traditional tales say that the form into which a character is transformed relates in some way to the person's behavior or personality.

ONCE UPON A TIME there was a beautiful girl who had a very cruel step-mother. One day, when the stepmother was leaving the house to go out, she put a bowl of delicious figs on the table and told the girl not to touch any of the figs or she would kill her. After a while, the poor, hungry girl took one of the figs and ate it.

Soon the stepmother returned, and the first thing she did was to go to the table to see if any of the figs that she had left were missing. Immediately she noticed that one fig was gone and asked the girl who had taken the fig from the bowl. The poor girl, very frightened, told her stepmother that she had taken the fig because she was very hungry. Full of anger, the stepmother went to kill the young girl and buried her in the backyard just as she had said she would do.

A short time later the father returned home and asked his wife about the miss-ing child. The stepmother, very afraid because of what she had done, told him the girl had gone to the forest. When the father sat down to eat, he looked out the win-dow and saw a beautiful fig tree growing in the backyard.

"Oh, how beautiful that fig tree is!" said the father to the stepmother. "Bring one of those delicious figs to me so I can eat it."

The stepmother went to the backyard, and when she was next to the fig tree she reached to take the most beautiful fig from the tree. But just as she placed her hand on the fig, she heard a mysterious song:

Mother, Mother
don't pull my hair
you have murdered me,
because I ate a fig.

The stepmother, frightened out of her wits, ran into the house to hide. The father, who had seen all that had happened but who had not heard the song, said to the wife: "I'll go and get a fig myself."

When the father stood near the fig tree to take a fig, he heard the sweet and lovely voice of his daughter singing:

Father, Father
don't pull my hair
my mother has killed me
because I ate a fig

The father, then, realized what had happened and rushed into the house and threw the cruel stepmother out. He immediately returned to the backyard and dug up his daughter, who was still alive. And so the father and his beautiful daughter lived happily ever after.

REFLECTIONS: *What other stories do you know about wicked stepmothers and beautiful stepdaughters? Are stepmothers always mean? See if you can tell a story where the stepmother represents good instead of evil.*

DADDY MENTION'S ESCAPE

Several legends about Daddy Mention have been documented. This one, which takes place in Polk County, comes from the Works Progress Administration. It is probably related to the African American John and Old Marster stories where the Black character engages in a somewhat good-humored battle of wits with the Old Marster, or the man who holds him in bondage. The slave, or in this case, the prisoner, always wins. In telling these stories, the more brutal circumstances of African Americans' lives are made visible.

This tale is told by one of Daddy Mention's fellow prisoners.

DADDY MENTION liked the Polk County jails alright, all except the little punishment box outside the Lakeland jail. He told the jailers that when they put him there, he didn't think he could stay with them too long.

They had locked him up for vagrancy, you see. And Daddy Mention didn't think too much of that, because just like he had told them, he had been picking oranges, and just had too much money to work for a week or two. He tried to tell them that he would go back to work as soon as he got broke, but you know you can't say much in Polk County.

So they locked Daddy Mention up; they gave him ninety days, straight up. That's ninety days with no time off for good behavior.

It was afternoon when Daddy Mention started to work, and he made the first day all right. He fussed a little, kind of under his breath, when he saw what the prisoners ate for supper. But he didn't say much out loud. The next morning he ate breakfast—grits and bacon grease, but without any bacon—with the rest of us, and went out to the woods.

Before it was ten o'clock—you know you have to start work at six in Polk County—Captain Smith had cussed at Daddy Mention two or three times. He didn't work fast enough to suit him. So when we went in for lunch, Daddy Mention was growling at the table. "They ain't treatin' me right," he said.

After lunch, when we lined up to go back to the woods to work, Captain Smith walked over to Daddy Mention. "Boy," he mostly hollered, "you gonna work this afternoon, or do you want to go into the punishment box?"

Daddy Mention didn't say anything at first. Then kinda slow he said, "Whatever you want me to do, Captain."

Captain Smith didn't know what to make of that, but it made him mad, so he put Daddy Mention in the box in a hurry. He didn't go back for him that day either. He didn't go back until the next day.

"You think you want to come out of there and work now, Boy?" he asked Daddy Mention, and Daddy Mention told him again, "Whatever you want me to do, Captain."

I didn't see Captain Smith then, but they tell me he got so hot you could fry eggs on him. He slammed the punishment box shut, and didn't go back for Daddy Mention for another day.

Daddy Mention didn't get out then either. Every day Captain Smith asked him the same thing, and every day Daddy Mention said the same thing.

Finally Captain Smith figured that maybe Daddy Mention wasn't trying to be smart, but was just dumb that way. So one day he let Daddy Mention come out. He sent him off to work with another gang of prisoners, the tree-chopping gang, working just ahead of us.

Daddy Mention was glad to get out, 'cause he had made up his mind to go to Tampa. He told some of the gang members about it when his Captain wasn't listening. But Daddy Mention knew he couldn't just run away. You can't do that in Polk County. They'd have you back in jail before you got as far as Mulberry. Daddy Mention knew he had to have a better plan, so he made one up.

We started seeing him do more work than anyone else in his gang. He could chop a big tree down all by himself, and it would take but one more man to help him lift it up on the pile. One day, when he was sure his captain saw him, he lifted one all by himself and carried it a long ways before he put it down.

The Captain didn't believe any man could grab one of those big pines and lift it up all by himself, much less carry it around. So he called to Daddy Mention and told him to do it again. He called to some of the other guards so they could see him do it too. Daddy Mention picked up another big tree all by himself, carried it a ways, and lifted it up onto the tree pile.

It wasn't long before the Captain and his friends started picking up a little side money by betting other people that Daddy Mention could pick up any tree they could cut. And they didn't fuss so much when Daddy Mention made a couple of nickels for himself.

So it got to be a regular sight to see Daddy Mention walking about the jail yard

carrying a big tree in his arms. Everybody was getting used to it. That was just what Daddy Mention wanted.

One afternoon we came in from the woods, and Daddy Mention was bringing a tree-butt with him. The Captain thought one of the other guards must have told him to bring it in, and didn't ask him anything about it.

Daddy Mention took his tree-butt to the dining room and stood it up by the wall. He then went on in with the rest of us and ate his dinner. He didn't seem to be in any hurry, but he didn't have much to say.

After dinner he waited until nearly everybody had finished. He then got up slowly and went back to his log. Most of the Captains and guards were around the yard then, and all of them watched while Daddy Mention picked up that big log.

Daddy Mention clowned around in front of the guards for a minute, then started towards the gate with the log on his shoulder. None of the guards bothered him because who ever saw a man escape with a tree-butt on his shoulder? You know, you have to pass the guard's quarters before you get to the gate in the Lakeland jail. But Daddy Mention didn't even turn around when he passed it, and nobody said anything to him. The guards must of thought the other guards sent him somewhere with the log, or was making a bet, or something.

Right on out the gate Daddy Mention went, and onto the road that goes to Hillsborough County. He still had the log on his shoulder. I never saw him again until a long time after in Tampa. I never did figure out how he got into Hillsborough County from Polk, with watchers all along the road, after he left the Lakeland jail. So I asked him.

"I didn't have any trouble," he told me. "I just kept that log on my shoulder, and everybody I passed thought it had fallen off a truck, and I was carrying it back. They knew no one would have nerve enough to steal a good pine log like that and walk along the highway with it. They didn't even bother me when I got out of Polk County. But soon as I got to Plant City, I took my log to a little wood yard and sold it. Then I had enough money to ride to Tampa."

Then Daddy Mention leaned back in a thoughtful manner and said, "They ain't going to catch me in Polk County ever again."

REFLECTIONS: *Describe what kind of man you think Daddy Mention was. How do you think he got to be so crafty? What would you think if you saw a man carrying a large log along a Florida highway?*

6

Ghosts and the Supernatural

Folklorist Jerrilyn McGregory observed that the Gothic South is so rich in narrative and literary traditions of the supernatural that it can be called "the world's most bedeviled region." In the Wiregrass region residents seem to take a respectful approach to the supernatural world, accommodating their religious understandings. People in this area believe that "all things are possible" (McGregory 79).

Many other places in Florida are known for their hauntings, ghost stories, and tales of the supernatural. For example, Saint Augustine is a popular ghost town where Dave Lapham easily collected numerous ghost tales for his book, *Ghosts of St. Augustine*. Newspaper reporter Tom Lowe claimed that since Saint Augustine is the oldest city in the United States, it has the oldest ghosts. Consequently, those who want to take a nightly walk with a storyteller can hear about ghosts that inhabit the Castillo de San Marcos, the fort the Spanish began building in 1672, or the ghosts that are frequently seen in the Huguenot Cemetery near the fort. The top floor of the Don Pedro Horruytiner House is said to be full of ghosts. While the owners of this house never go upstairs, it is said that the curtains are sometimes open, sometimes closed. The developer Henry Flagler is another ghost who is often sighted in the college that was named for him. Other stories of ghosts and supernatural experiences abound in this historic town.[1]

Perhaps an even better-known Florida ghost town is Cassadaga, the oldest religious community in the southeastern United States. Over a hundred years old, the town began as a winter community for Spiritualists. Spiritualism, most prevalent in the nineteenth century, was practiced by such people as Harriet Beecher Stowe, Mary Todd Lincoln, and Sojourner Truth. Spiritualists believe that they can provide evidence of religious truth and that this evidence appears when a medium channels messages through spirit guides. Visitors come from all over the world to get "read-ings" from Cassadaga's psychics.[2] If one sits on the porch of Cassadaga's Davis Build-ing for a short time, as I have often done, one can hear all kinds of tales. Disbeliev-ers may consider such tales superstitions or delusions, but Spiritualists refer to them as evidence of the fact that we never die and only pass on to another state of being. In the time I have spent doing fieldwork there, I have heard stories about the Cas-sadaga Hotel and other houses in town being haunted. One of my students tells a tale about a trip he made to the graveyard that ended in the motor of his truck mys-teriously dying, only to start again the following morning after an uneasy night spent in the cemetery. In Cassadaga, the spirits of those who have passed on routinely appear.

But apparitions can be seen in many other places besides Cassadaga. Jack San-tino reports many pilots and attendants, numerous in Florida, tell stories about see-ing images of pilots of planes that have crashed. Often they appear in order to warn of an impending disaster. While these tales are not typically told to the public, in private situations, they are quietly repeated.[3]

Ghosts appear to people for many different reasons. Sometimes they intend to be helpful, as is the case with the pilot ghosts. Other times they intend to frighten those they come in contact with, but they do it with humor. Ghosts found in the Wiregrass region, for example, tend not to be terribly vindictive but lurk rather harmlessly around abandoned buildings. When the teller uses humor relating the tale, tension is relieved, and some normalcy returns to the setting. The listener has an opportunity to refocus on the everyday (McGregory 74–75).

Ghosts can also appear in many different ways. They may not actually be seen, but reportedly sometimes can be heard or sensed. If they are invisible, they may sim-ply create mischief by moving things or opening and closing doors to indicate their presence. Sometimes a smell signals the presence of a ghost. When they are seen, they may appear in various ways, generally in the manner in which they looked when they died.[4] Ghosts are often connected to specific places, often the place where someone died.

Almost everyone seems to enjoy a good ghost story. Even Carl Jung, the famous psychiatrist, was intrigued by ghosts and the supernatural. He was open to all kinds of possibilities of explaining things, and it is even said that he was open to inves-tigative reports of manifestations such as flying saucers. One tale told about him is that he argued vigorously with Charles Lindbergh when Lindbergh suggested that they couldn't exist.[5]

Whether one truly believes that ghosts and supernatural experiences can be real or not is basically irrelevant for the tale to be successful. If the tale is a good one, and the teller is successful, at some level we become engaged enough in the story that the possibility exists that the tale might have truth in it. In fact, we cannot be sure if the tale is "merely" fiction and whether its time and place are securely in the past. We often ask ourselves if the event might be now occurring or possible in a future context.[6]

Folk beliefs often lay the groundwork for tales about ghosts and the supernatural. These kinds of beliefs (sometimes referred to as superstitions) can be incorporated into the tale or can help set the stage for our attraction and participation in the narrative. For instance, many of us may intellectually believe that walking under a ladder or opening an umbrella inside the house is not going to bring us bad luck, but we probably wouldn't do it anyway—just in case.

Florida is full of folk beliefs related to ghosts and the supernatural. Many were recorded in the WPA *Negro Guides*. These include the notion that babies born with cauls (also known as veils) over their eyes have supernatural power, such as being able to heal others or see ghosts. Likewise, if a baby is born near midnight, it is said that that child will have the ability to see ghosts. If you see a ghost coming toward your house, it means that someone will become ill. If the ghost is going in the opposite direction, someone will die. If you are perturbed by repeated appearances of a ghost and you wish to see him disappear, swear at him and demand to know the purpose of his business. He will respond honestly and never bother you again. Horseshoes should be nailed over doors to ward off any impending bad luck and evil spirits (McDonogh 73–74).

Some horror stories are about ghosts of murdered people who come back to haunt the murderer in an effort to force a confession. The spirits are typically successful in their quest. However, Florida's African American lore claims that if you kill someone, it is a good idea to place the victim face down because then they can't haunt you. Sources from the *Negro Guide*, however, claim that this effort might very well have backfired on murderers, since this bit of folklore was so well known that it would point to an African American criminal (McDonogh 73).

Sometimes specific animals or birds are thought to bring signs of foreboding. In the Wiregrass region, owls are familiar figures in ghostly lore. They appear to warn of an impending death (McGregory 75). Some residents of this Panhandle region call people who have the skills to see ghosts "root doctors" who have a second sight; they have the ability to conjure (74). Roots and herbs are used by root doctors to heal and cure ailments. For example, the devil's shoestring can be placed around the neck to ward off bad luck and evil spirits. In the late 1930s and early '40s, there was a conjure shop in Jacksonville where African Americans would go to get roots and herbs from a root doctor. It was a referred to as a small "hole in the wall" located in the 400 block of Broad Street (McDonogh 86–87).

During slavery times, some bondswomen were reported to be conjurers who could use their powers for either good or evil. They would boast about their talents, which included either casting or removing unwanted spells, predicting the future, and brewing potions that encouraged lovemaking (White 135).

This last section of this book contains many kinds of ghost sightings. Some of the tales are humorous, and some are just plain frightening. One tale is about a witch. While this tale is Bahamian and comes from South Florida, it is interesting to note that McGregory documented a very similar tale in the Wiregrass region. It was told by an African American undertaker from Cairo, Georgia. This tale also included a cat, but the apparition was of a dead aunt instead of a sister-in-law (74).

The category of witches has been understood in various ways. McNeil claims that witches differ from ghosts because they are living people with supernatural powers, whereas ghosts represent the dead (10). However, in the Bahamian tale told here, and in the Wiregrass version, the witch represents a person who has passed away. It is important to note that the term *witch* was historically used to describe women who were killed for their "eccentric practices" in the fifteenth through the seventeenth centuries. Mary Daly claims that nine million people were put to death in this mass genocide of women who cured with herbs and ritualistic practices (183–205).[7]

Not all the tales of ghosts and the supernatural in this section may appeal to you. But they are all grounded in Florida's cultural lore. You may want to tell them around a campfire, at night with a candle burning, or at any late-night gathering. The darkness helps create the mood.

THE ST. ANDREWS BAY LEGEND

This is a tale that took place around Panama City in the Panhandle. It was documented in the late 1930s.

IN THE EARLY DAYS of Florida's settlement, a bolt of calico cloth was considered a very important possession. One settler was transporting a bolt of calico to his home, where Panama City now stands. Two Indians saw him walking, and they followed him for a distance. After some time passed, the settler discovered the Indians following him. It was then that the Indians attacked. They fired their stolen rifles at the White man carrying the calico. But the bolt of calico stopped the bullets quite effectively, and the White settler was saved from death. In order to rid himself of his attackers, the settler pretended to have been shot. The Indians ran to where he lay to get the bolt of cloth. The White man rose up and slew one red man with a knife, and the other fled. Today, from time to time, the ghost of the slain Indian is seen walking along the beach of St. Andrews Bay, dressed in calico garments.

REFLECTIONS: *Why do you think calico cloth was so valued during the early days of Florida's settlement? What do you think the White man intended to do with it? What would the Indians have done with it? Do you think this is a story passed down in the Indian community or a tale told in the White community? Why do you think so?*

THE WITCH

The image of the witch can be traced back at least to the fourteenth century in Europe. All children know that witches can be scary. Witches are most often women and, in folklore, have most often been portrayed as wicked. However, some storytellers now depict witches as wise women who were persecuted unfairly.

This story, told in South Florida, takes place in the Bahamas and follows the old-fashioned idea of the witch as someone to fear. Stetson Kennedy recorded it sometime between 1937 and 1942. Since most of Florida's residents come from other places, the stories they tell are often about events that took place in their homeland.

IT USED TO BE that when I was living in the Bahamas, I never stayed home alone, especially at night when my husband had gone to sea on one of his fishing trips. But this time, that I'm about to explain to you, is one time when my babies and me were left home without anybody else around. That's when I was awful young and my children were just little ones. My girl, who still lives with me, was the littlest one.

The whole event that came about was like this. As I said before, I didn't want to stay alone, but it just couldn't be helped. I took all the bedclothes off the bed, and I made myself a place to rest on the floor near the front door. This was so I could get some fresh air where it would be cooler.

You know, in the Bahamas, folks just don't sleep with the house open. In fact, they usually bar all the windows and doors, for they think that the night air is foul. Well, I knew better than that. This night the air was fresh. Besides, this night I was scared, so I preferred being near the door. That way I could see if someone was coming. I put a lamp right near my head so that I could see all around me. Then my babies and me lay down to sleep. The children when right off to sleep, but me, I just laid there awake for a while.

Then, first thing I knew, I heard a bump up on the ridgepole of the house. Of course, all the houses in the Bahamas have thatched roofs, and one can see from the floor clean to the rooftop on the inside. I never thought much about the noise, but I also heard it clawing around up there in the thatch. I just figured it was our cat, so I didn't pay it any mind.

Then, again without thinking, I happened to glance up, and there on the ridge pole, and peeking through the thatch, was the biggest black cat I ever seen. But being sleepy I still figured it was my own cat, and I still didn't pay it any mind. It just sat there looking down at me and grinning.

Then once more without thinking, I happened to glance across the room and saw my own tabby cat sleeping on a window sill. Well, by this time I thought I was crazy or seeing things, and I looked first at one cat and then at the other, but both were still there. And I noticed then what I should have noticed before, but hadn't. That cat up on the ridge pole was much bigger than my own, and he was just as black as midnight. And there he was still sitting there staring down at me. I was frightened by that time and started to get up. When I did, he disappeared.

I was a bit shook up, but I laid back down again and tried to go off to sleep. In fact, I had almost forgotten the whole cat experience when I heard the rusty hinge of my bedroom door squeak. The door was right near my head, but I had to turn to see what the noise was. I had to turn quite a bit, but I just figured that it was the breeze blowing the door. But it wasn't the breeze. There, by my bedroom door, was the worst looking little Black woman I have ever seen in my life! She was the size of a midget, and she had the funniest mouth I ever saw on anybody; it almost covered her whole face. She just stood there grinning at me like that cat up in the ridge pole had been doing. Her body—if she had one—was covered with rags, and they fluttered in the faint breeze.

Well I know that this story sounds like it isn't true, but it sure is, and if God himself was to come along right now, I'd tell him the same thing.

I was so scared at what I saw that I just froze; I couldn't move. No, dear, I couldn't move an inch. I wanted to yell and I couldn't; I wanted to run, and I couldn't do that neither. The babies hadn't awakened so I was all alone to face that old hag, all by myself.

After standing and staring at me for a bit, she came out of the room and began to walk circles around my bedclothes. I was still so frightened I couldn't do anything but watch. You know, not only was she terrifying to look at, she didn't have any feet either, and if she did they were hidden inside the rags she wore. As she came moving past me, she just floated on thin air.

About this time my babies woke up, and they started watching her too. You must understand that I was still so frozen that I couldn't open my mouth. I didn't do anything but watch until the witch reached down and tried to grab the leg of my baby. She's the girl who lives with me now. Remember I told you that she was the youngest then? When that hag touched my baby, it was like I found my voice, and I started hollering loud. I got up to my feet too, ready to protect my baby, but when I did, the witch disappeared.

I've never seen her since, and I hope I will never see anything like her again. I just figured it was my sister-in-law, my brother's wife, who had died just a few days before, and she came back to haunt us. And that's the only explanation I have.

REFLECTIONS: *Do you find this tale scary or humorous? Why? Was the ending a surprise? Have you heard any similar kinds of stories before where the character sees someone who has just died? How does this witch compare with other witches you have heard or read about?*

HUGGING MOLLY

Sometimes when tales are passed on, new characteristics are added. Often the new versions are told so that they take place in the storyteller's locale. Here are two versions of a similar story.

THE CHARACTER WE NOW call Hugging Molly came from West Florida. Molly Cottontail was her full name. She was a tall, angular Indian woman who lived in a hut on the hill all alone. She wore rags that hung down behind her into the trails. This is why they called her "Cottontail." She always had an old clay pipe in her mouth and a long stick in her hand. They say that she caught young children, carried them to her hut, and hugged them till it hurt. For this, she was called "The Hugging Molly."

Another version of this tale comes from Saint Augustine, in East Florida. This rendition tells of a stone called the "Molly Stone."

Long ago there lived an old lady who was very poor. She had no relatives, and she constantly visited a special stone. Friends said she wandered there at night. One very cold night she made her usual visit, and the next morning she was found frozen

to death near the stone. The people in that neighborhood claim she still visits the stone every night, and
as travelers pass there is something in the air that
seems to hug them.

REFLECTIONS: *What are the similarities and
differences in these two stories? Do you think they
are related? Can you imagine how one story
might have been told again and again, eventually to become the other? Which one do
you like best and why? Can you tell a third
version about Hugging Molly?*

MYSTIC MUSIC OF THE MANATEES

*This legend was documented in the 1930s. Legends usually have some historical ele-
ment of truth and are often set in a particular location. They often also contain some
supernatural events, as this one does. In this case, there may have been an early ship-
wreck in the Manatee River. Specific people are sometimes named in legends, making
them more believable.*

THIS INDIAN LEGEND may seem incredible to many who visit the Braden-
town, Palmetto, and Manatee area today. But the pioneer settlement of Manatee
was subject, even 90 years ago, to a soothing hum in the tidal waters of the Manatee
River. To the new settlers, the crooning, whispering, and washing-in of the full tidal

waters was a marvelous event. The sound that came from the waters was like a beautiful song. But to the Seminoles, who knew the river well, it was the home of spirits, and the haunting, mysterious melody was the "Mystic Music of the Manatee." They knew this to be true because the legend had been passed down to them from the ancient Calusa Indians who lived in the vicinity of Manatee before the Colombian period, when the sounds began.

The legend tells us that many years ago, a strange ship with huge wings came gliding up the river as if in great fear. Soon, other ships followed in swift pursuit, and those watching on shore saw many strange packages dropped off the sides of the leading vessel. A beautiful woman with long, yellow, flowing hair appeared. In her hand she held a strange object from which she drew strange and lovely sounds. As the craft sank below the surface of the river, she still played as if to warn away all trespassers. Each year in the dark of the moon in May, she is heard again. The mournful notes of the golden-haired maiden that filled the air as she sank beneath the waves are repeated again and again. It is said that she plays to guard the treasure still buried at the bottom of the Manatee River.

From the ancient Calusa Indians, through the Seminoles, who related the legend to the Manatee County pioneer settlers, this was recorded and is remembered today because Miss Eva Gates, granddaughter of the pioneer Josiah Gates passed it on to us. When we first heard it, Miss Gates was teaching school in Manatee County.

Since the dredging of the river many, many years ago, the music is not so loud as before, according to listeners. But it still can be heard faintly, softly—the same mysterious musical notes.

REFLECTIONS: *Can you tell this story by filling in some of the missing pieces? For example, what was the treasure? Who was on the ships? Who is the musical maiden and why is she protecting the treasure? What object did she use to make music?*

FIVE-MILE BANK

Almost every state has a story about a lovers' leap. Typically, as is true here, they are Indian lovers. These kinds of tales are often used to encourage people to visit tourist sites, where people say that one of the grieving lovers can sometimes be sighted.

ONCE, LONG AGO, there lived a tribe of Indians on the Five-Mile Bank. With this tribe lived a beautiful Indian princess, who was in love with a young warrior of the same tribe. During an attack on another tribe, the young warrior was killed. When she received news of her lover's death, the young maiden pined away bit by bit. Finally, one day, she grew so lonely that she ran and threw herself off the bank at the Five-Mile, which was then very steep. Nothing was ever heard of her after that, although some say that there are times when she comes and sits on the beach, and there she cries all night long for her lost lover. But it may be merely the wind blowing in the trees.

REFLECTIONS: *Do you know a story similar to this one? Can you tell it?*

THE ARMORED GHOST

Many of Pensacola's local legends are about old Spaniards who are often called Juan. In this case, Juan becomes a ghost who is seen locally. Generally speaking, ghosts appear because of some unfinished business, which seems to apply in this case.

While this is a tale about an individual experience, there is a history of unrest in Florida between some Indian groups and the Spaniards. In fact, Southern Indians fought, at various times, against the European powers and among each other. The killings represented here could be reflective of numerous conflicts.

A repeated theme in ghost stories has to do with someone being trapped somewhere, and in this case the victim is not able to get out of a tree. Ghost stories are often applied to specific places, and in "The Armored Ghost," a few names of places are mentioned. This folktale was published by the Pensacola Historical Society in 1990.

JUAN ALVERADO, a Spanish soldier who had been stationed in Havana, Cuba, was transferred to Pensacola. When he kissed his sweetheart in Cuba goodbye, he did not know if he would ever see her again.

One day Juan and a friend were exploring the Escambia River. Several Indians, who were supposedly friendly, guided them. But the Indians turned on the Spaniards when they got to Cottage Hill Landing. They killed Juan's friend and mortally wounded Juan, who hid in a hollow cypress tree. He did not have the strength to get out of the tree when the danger was over. Juan died inside the cypress tree.

In later years, settlers in the area reported seeing an armored ghost, who would come out once a year, wander around at sunset and then disappear. When the tree was cut down in 1929, it split open when it fell and revealed a skeleton wearing a suit of armor. The skeleton was buried in a Pensacola cemetery, and the armored ghost has not been seen since.

REFLECTIONS: *In this tale, there does not seem to be any direct connection between Juan saying good-bye to his sweetheart in Cuba and the rest of the story except for the fact that he was never to see her again. Can you retell the story so that a stronger connection is made between Juan and his sweetheart?*

THE WOMAN WHO FED HER HUSBAND A LEG WHICH SHE DUG UP FROM A CEMETERY

Sometimes ghost stories can be gruesome. This horror story about dismemberment comes from the Library of Congress. Part of the story collection from the Works Progress Administration, it was recorded in Ybor City on August 23, 1939, by Robert Cook and Stetson Kennedy. The teller is Ziomara Andux. It was recorded in Spanish and translated by Maria Redmon.

Those who return from the dead are sometimes called "returners" or "revenants." A common theme for a story about a dismembered ghost is a return either to seek revenge or to get back the missing body part. This is the kind of tale that has haunted generations of children for hundreds of years.

ONCE UPON A TIME there was a woman who lived with her husband far from town near the forest. One day they were getting ready for a party, and the husband brought home a pig for supper. The husband had to go to town to buy bread for the party, so the wife went to the kitchen to prepare the food. She was very hungry and could not wait for dinner to eat, so she ate the pig.

After she had eaten the pig, she realized that she had to find food for her guests. Suddenly, she thought of a way to feed her guests. She went to the cemetery, dug up a dead man and cut off a leg. She brought the leg home. At once she started to cook it and prepare it for her guests, for they were to be there soon.

After her husband and her guests arrived, she set the food on the table, and everyone began to eat. But the woman could not take a bite of food. She knew what she had cooked, and all she could do was watch in horror as her guests ate. Late that night, after all of her guests had left, she went to bed.

She tried to sleep, but could not. A voice kept calling out to her:

I'm around the corner. Give me back my leg.
I'm at the front door. Give me back my leg.

I'm in the living room. Give me back my leg.
I'm in the kitchen. Give me back my leg.
I'm in your bedroom. Give me YOUR LEG!
I'm next to your bed. NOW I'VE GOT YOU! AHA!

REFLECTIONS: *Have you heard this story, or one like it, before? Why would a ghost need a leg? When and where is the best time to tell a story like this one?*

A GHOST STORY ABOUT AN AUNT

The Federal Writers Project put many out-of-work folklorists and writers to work in the 1930s and '40s. They collected a variety of stories throughout Florida. This one is based on a story tape-recorded by Robert Cook and Stetson Kennedy in January 1940. It is found in the Folklore Archives in the Library of Congress.

Eartha White, who lived in Jacksonville, told it with the kind of enjoyment her mother must have passed on to her. While this story is about a ghost it is not as frightening as many ghost stories are. This humorous tale invites speculation.

THIS IS A TRUE STORY my Mother liked to tell. During the days of slavery, my mother was a house girl on a plantation on Amelia Island, which is off Florida's east coast near the Georgia border. She was born there. It is about an event she witnessed since she was there when it happened. This was an actual incident that took place some time before the Civil War.

While dinner was being served, in the early evening, one of the family members raced home in a Panic—he almost fell off his horse. He ran into the house and fell onto the floor. He startled everybody. When he calmed down and came to be more like himself, he began to tell about an experience he had just had on the road.

He said that as he was coming down the big road, just as he got near the cemetery, his aunt stopped his horse. She had owned the horse during her lifetime, but she had passed away some time before. But there she was.

At first, the horse seemed to recognize her voice, and it stood at attention. But the man said that when he heard his aunt speak, every strand of his hair stood on end. And then he heard someone stroking the horse. And she said to the man, calling him by name, "Don't be afraid." She said, "I want you to meet me tomorrow, at sundown." And then she told him exactly where she would be. She continued, "I have something for you. I am your aunt. Meet me tomorrow at sundown. I am your aunt. I have something for you."

Right when she finished talking, the horse got frightened, and the man became more afraid than ever. So he ran home, stumbled up the steps, and fell into the dining room. He frightened everyone else with the look on his face and the panic in his voice. And when he calmed down, they said to him, "Certainly, you are going to meet her, hear what she has to say, and get whatever it is she has to give you?"

But the man, startled by his family's response, replied, "Not me! She can keep whatever it is she has. I won't be there!"

This is a real story, and my mother always delighted in repeating it.

REFLECTIONS: *What do you think the aunt had for her nephew? Can you continue the story making it end in a scary way? Why did the horse stay calm at first, but later get frightened? Why do you think the family responded the way they did? Would you have gone to meet the aunt?*

A CHRISTMAS GHOST STORY

While folklore is generally passed on orally, sometimes traditional stories are kept alive through the media. This Pensacola tale was first published in the Pensacola Journal *in December 15, 1907. The teller is an elderly man who relays an experience he witnessed in his early years.*

In this story, the ghost is a bearer of bad tidings. This is a figure that often appears in tales from Wales, Scotland, and Ireland and is sometimes referred to as a banshee. The word in Gaelic means "fairy woman" and is thought of as a death spirit. Her eyes are often bright from continual weeping. The banshee can appear to be beautiful but is also described as having only one nostril, a protruding front tooth and drooping breasts. In states besides Florida, these kinds of experiences have been reported in local newspapers as a matter of news.

NEARLY SIXTY YEARS AGO, there lived in Pensacola an old gentleman named Jarlier. He was an ex-officer of the French navy who had resigned from that service and first settled in Mobile or New Orleans, where he married into one of the French Creole families.

His wife, who was much younger than himself, had evidently been very pretty in her youth. When I knew her, she was middle-aged and somewhat broken by years of hard work and poverty. Nonetheless, she was cheerful in spite of her cares. She had but one thought in her life, and that was to care for her husband, whom she idolized.

Mr. Jarlier was a man whom no one could have known without loving. Handsome and dignified in appearance, graceful in his movements, with gentle and courtly manners and refined speech, he won the regard and interest of everyone with whom he came into contact. He supported his wife and himself by giving instructions in the French language, and as Pensacola then offered only a few interested pupils, his earnings were scanty. But Madame Jarlier did all of her own household work, and with the careful management and economy of a French woman, she made her husband's earnings sufficient for content and comfort.

Some years after their settlement in Pensacola, the health of Mr. Jarlier failed and he went into a gradual decline.

At that time I was employed in the county and was able to travel home only on Sundays and holidays. I came home one Christmas Eve, the 24th of December. After supper my mother said to me, "Son, let's go down the street and see our old friend, Mr. Jarlier. We'll take him a little Christmas present."

She filled a basket with cakes and fruit and handed it to me and we went out together.

The Jarliers were living in a cottage on Baylen Street. As we entered, we found bright fire on the hearth, and Mr. Jarlier in bed, looking worn and ill but as courteous and pleasant as ever.

My mother offered him her little present, which was accepted with thanks. She then turned to talk with Madame Jarlier, but the poor woman seemed much dis-

tressed and troubled. She answered my mother's questions in monosyllables—and occasionally wiped her eyes. At length, my mother said to her, "Madame, you seem to be in trouble. Is there anything the matter or can I do anything to help you?"

"Oh no, Madame," she cried, breaking down entirely, while the tears streamed down her face. "But I saw a ghost last night."

"My poor friend," said my mother soothingly. "There is no such thing as a ghost. You are tired and anxious, and you had a bad dream."

"Oh no, Madame," she said. "Let me tell you. I was sitting here last night just as I am now. My Jarlier was in his bed asleep and no one was with me. I was wide-awake and the fire burned bright. All of a sudden I felt cold, as if the door was open. I turned around and I saw a beautiful lady all dressed in white standing by Mr. Jarlier's bed. She wrung her hands together this way, and said, 'Poor Mr. Jarlier. In two months he will die.' And then she was gone. I was frightened. I got up and went to look at Mr. Jarlier and found him to be sound asleep.

"So I think to myself, maybe it is a bad dream, and I go back and sit down and put some more wood on the fire. After a while, all of a sudden, I feel cold again. I look and see the same lady standing by Mr. Jarlier's bed. She is crying and wringing her hands together and she says to me, 'Poor Mr. Jarlier. In two months he will die.' And then she was gone.

"I tremble all over. Again I go to the bed and look at Mr. Jarlier and he is still sleeping like a child. Then I go down on my knees and make my prayers to the good God to have mercy upon us and to take care of us. I then go back and sit by the fire.

"After a time, I feel the cold once again, and I look up and see the same lady standing by the bed. She is crying and wringing her hands together and she says to me, 'Poor Mr. Jarlier. In two months he will die." And then she is gone.

"I jump up and run to the bed and I take a hold of Mr. Jarlier. He wakes up and asks me what the matter is. And I tell him. He replies, 'Oh my dear wife, you are tired and you have had bad dreams. Come and lie down by me and try to rest.'

"So I creep into the bed by him and he soon falls asleep again. But I, I do not sleep. I say my prayers and I cry as I lie there. Oh Madame, it is no dream. I was awake and I saw that lady three times as plain as I see you and she was always the same."

The poor soul broke down again in an agony of weeping. My mother comforted and soothed her as well as she was able. After a while, we bade them goodnight and left them.

We visited them afterwards, at intervals, but allusion was never made to Madame Jarlier's painful experience, and the impression seemed to fade away. Mr. Jarlier grew weaker and weaker. But he was a man of the most sincere piety, and he always greeted us with a smile and words of courtesy, so that we felt elevated by contact with so refined and gentle a spirit.

I came home one evening in February. Some member of my family said to me, "Your old friend, Mr. Jarlier, died since you were last here."

"When did he die?" I asked.

"He died last Wednesday, the 23rd," was the reply.

My mother and I looked at each other. It was exactly two months from the date of Madame Jarlier's vision.

REFLECTIONS: *Do you think this story is more apt to be true because it was reported in a newspaper? Would you be likely to read this kind of story in your local newspaper? Why or why not?*

NOTES

INTRODUCTION

1. Findlay and Bing quote Evenell Powell-Brant as saying, "There never was a master list. No local lists survive—indeed if there ever were any. Only by grapevine reports and recollections do we know who did the work" (p. 292).

2. For a more complete discussion on how illustrations can enhance the storytelling process, see Marantz et al.

1. TELLING TRADITIONAL TALES IN FLORIDA

1. This list of names was found in Goss.

2. This idea relates to another passage found in McDonogh from the early 1940s: "Tunes, tales and characters are still emerging" (xx). This idea holds true today.

3. This song has been controversial in recent years because many of Florida's residents feel that it is racist. From time to time there is discussion about selecting a new official state song.

4. While controlled burning has been outlawed in Florida, it is now being reconsidered as an ecologically balanced way to sustain the environment.

5. McGregory quoted one resident as saying that the residents would "drink rum out of town and come in here and load up on good whiskey. . . . That would run them crazy and they were not used to any law. Naturally, when they were taught there must be law here, plenty of trouble followed" (p. 71).

6. Ste. Claire claims the tough cow towns began in Florida with the Spanish settlements in the 1500s and lasted until the open ranges closed in 1949. Florida was perhaps wilder than any "wild West" territory (16 and 178).

7. Padilla reported that Florida is now 15.4 percent Hispanic (2,334,000), 15.4 percent Black (2,333,000), 2.2 percent Asian and Native American (341,724), and 67 percent Non-Hispanic or White (10.2 million). Of course, one could easily question these statistics, as people are increasingly identifying themselves as racially mixed.

8. Burt devoted an entire chapter (36–54) to Norton Baskin, Rawling's second husband, who was a great storyteller in his own right. He knew Ernest Hemingway, Scott and Zelda Fitzgerald, Margaret Mitchell, and Maxwell Perkins and enjoyed talking about them. Rawlings often depended on Baskin to entertain guests with his many and varied tales.

9. Bucuvalas, Bulger, and Kennedy reported that alligator wrestling was never originally part of Seminole culture, but it was done for economic reasons to increase tourist trade (218–19). Interestingly, there has recently been dialogue on a folklore public sector listserve about an item from a local Florida newspaper that stated "Indian tribe seeks alligator wrestlers." Reportedly,

Seminole tribe spokesperson Cuck Malkus said, "Traditionally, Seminoles have done this. . . . The reason why we have the job openings is because tribe members now are going into banking, communications, e-commerce and law school, so we have a shortage of candidates." (Tina Bucuvalas, Sept. 8, 2000, *publore@listserv.nmmnh-abq.mus.nm.us*).

10. According to Ammidown, the girls in antebellum costumes were added to the garden when a 1940s freeze killed off many of the plants, leaving unsightly holes in the garden displays. Visitors were so delighted in the addition of the young girls that they were made a permanent addition after the plants grew back (252).

2. HOW THINGS CAME TO BE THE WAY THEY ARE

1. Explaining how these definitions affect us, Allen states: "The current dictionary definitions of myth reinforce a bias that enables the current paradigm of our technocratic social science-biased society to prevail over tribal or poetic views just as it enables an earlier Christian biblical paradigm as prevailing over the pagan one."

2. See Allen's book for more justification on the topic of mythology and moral insight.

3. This bit of folklore was told to me by Tina Bucuvalas, Florida's state folklorist.

3. PEOPLE WITH SPECIAL POWERS

1. In reality, Johnny Appleseed was not exactly the character he is portrayed to be. See Richard M. Dorson, *American Folklore* (Chicago: University of Chicago Press, 1959), 232–36, where he describes Appleseed as a successful businessman who owned twenty-two properties of nearly twelve thousand acres.

2. Bucuvalas, Bulger, and Kennedy, in their book *South Florida Folklore*, report that Remington made a few paintings of Florida's cowmen. He commented that they "lack dash and are indifferent riders, but they are picturesque in their unkempt, almost unearthly wildness" (40). For information on how the cowboy or cowman has been portrayed in relationship to the landscape, see Furlong's "Landscape as Cinema." She wrote about the paintings and sculptures of Frederic Remington and how they were instrumental in shaping our understanding of the Western landscape as empty, brutal, and harsh. Those who were able to survive it were brave and strong. While the focus here is on the West, some conclusions could also be made about Remington's work with Bone Mizell and Florida's landscape.

3. The best known teller of Bone Mizell tales is Jim Bob Tinsley, who wrote *Florida Cow Hunter: The Life and Times of Bone Mizell*. The versions of the tales told here are from Tinsley, who is the second inductee into the National Cowboy Song and Poetry Hall of Fame. Tinsley lives in Ocala, Florida, and Brevard, North Carolina. He also wrote the classic book *He Was Singin' This Song* (Orlando: University of Central Florida Press, 1981).

4. Jerrilyn McGregory's book *Wiregrass Country*, 78, includes a memory from Bessie Jones, a member of the Sea Island Singers, who knew a snake charmer who had some kind of "funny stuff on him." He blew a strange instrument and "the snakes came right around him as though he had called chickens that were his pets. They came up and wrapped themselves around him, all around his neck, and he would just grab one, jerk its mouth open and put his hand in there and pull out that bag. . . . He got about 48 out of the woods."

5. McGregory suggested that it may be no accident that snake roundups became more popular in the 1960s when residents were restricted in burning the grasslands (109).

6. See Bucuvalas, Bulger, and Kennedy (50–51) for other versions of this tale as well an analysis of other tales about the abundance of alligators hunted in one trip.

4. FOOD, FRIENDS, AND FAMILY

1. See Alvin Toffler's *The Third Wave* (44) on how families changed because of the Industrial Revolution.

5. UNUSUAL PLACES, SPACES, AND EVENTS

1. Thanks to Frank and Ann Thomas and Ann Hyman for this insight into Polk County humor. Each year, the Florida Humanities Council holds a Gathering somewhere in Florida. Much of the programming focuses on folklore.

2. For a more detailed description of Cassadaga see Brotemarkle 106–14. The belief about birds not flying over Cassadaga was told to me several times when doing research in Cassadaga from 1994 to 1998.

6. GHOSTS AND THE SUPERNATURAL

1. See Lapham for more ghost tales about this area. Sightings of ghosts are also discussed in Tom Lowe's article, "In Search of Oldest City's Ghosts."

2. For a discussion of Spiritualism, see Braude's *Radical Spirits*. Harriet Beecher Stowe, Mary Todd Lincoln, and Sojourner Truth are discussed on pages 27–29. For specific information on Cassadaga, see Brotemarkle 106–14.

3. Santino explained how important it is to the airplane industry that these tales not get out, given the fear many people have of flying. Santino also noted that these tales seem to become more prevalent at the time when workers are fired and they insist on the strength of these experiences in the field.

4. See McNeil 10. See McNeil for tales that illustrate a variety of ways of knowing that ghosts are present.

5. Brandon recounts this interaction between Lindbergh and Jung (253). She describes how Jung's open-mindedness helped him to formulate his doctrine of the collective unconscious. He apparently had an intellectual attraction to Spiritualism.

6. Stewart explains how a horror story can shift in time and space. She also details how the audience place themselves in the role of victim as the narrative unfolds.

7. How much current tales about witches relate to the mass killings of women who were identified as witches is debatable. What is clear is that the way witches are presented in folktales varies. For a detailed description of the genocide of witches in Western culture, see Daly.

SOURCES FOR TRADITIONAL TALES

HOW THINGS CAME TO BE THE WAY THEY ARE

"Why Men and Women Don't Have Tails Like Cows," "How the Gopher Turtle Was Made," "How Florida Got That Way," "Cape Sable Cats," "Why the Rabbit Is Wild Today," "Stolen Fire," "The Alligator and the Eagle," and "The Legend of the Moss" from Florida Writers' Project, Department of State, Division of Historical Resources, Florida Folklife Archives.

"Buzzard Roost" from Sandra Johnson, Leora Sutton, and the Pensacola Historical Society.

PEOPLE WITH SPECIAL POWERS

"Uncle Monday," "How to Handle a Rattlesnake," and "Old Pete" from Florida Writers' Project, Department of State, Division of Historical Resources, Florida Folklife Archives.

"Acrefoot Johnson" from Phyllis NeSmith. Thanks also to the Will McLean Foundation.

"Bone Mizell and His Teeth" and "Bone Mizell and the Circus" from Jim Bob Tinsley and the University Presses of Florida.

"Railroad Bill" from Sandra Johnson, Lenora Sutton, and the Pensacola Historical Society.

"The Turkey Maiden" from Ralph Steele Boggs, "Spanish Folklore from Tampa, Florida: (No. 5) Folktales," *Southern Folklore Quarterly* 2.1 (Mar. 1938): 87–106. Thanks also to Maria Redmon for her translation.

FOOD, FRIENDS, AND FAMILY

"Kerosene Charley and the Potatoes" and "The Shoemaker and the King" from Florida Writers' Project, Department of State, Division of Historical Resources, Florida Folklife Archives.

"The Little Boy and 'Ayayay'" from Liliane Nérette Louis and Libraries Unlimited/Teacher Ideas Press. Also thanks to the University Press of Mississippi and the version of this tale in *South Florida Folklife* by Tina Bucuvalas, Peggy Bulger, and Stetson Kennedy.

"Sister's Milkcow" and "Cutting a Pumpkin" from Richard Seaman in Gregory Hansen, "The Relevance of 'Authentic Tradition' in Studying an Oldtime Florida Fiddler," *Journal of Southern Folklore* 53.2 (1996): 86.

"Homer and the Bear" from Ada Forney.

"Grandpa and the Panther" from the Will McLean Foundation.

"The Preacher and the Ducks" from Phyllis NeSmith.

"Aunt Hazel" from Myra Davis.

"The Cucarachita Martinez" and "The Bunny Rabbit" from Ralph Steele Boggs, "Spanish

Folklore from Tampa, Florida: (No. 5) Folktales," *Southern Folklore Quarterly* 2.1 (Mar. 1938): 87–106. Thanks also to Maria Redmon for her translations.

"Uncle Luke" from Stephen Caldwell Wright.

UNUSUAL PLACES, SPACES, AND EVENTS

"My First Job" from Chuck Larkin.

"The Man and the Beanstalk," "Diddy-Wah-Diddy," "Old Frostysides," "Big John Gives Old Master a Sign," and "Daddy Mention's Escape" from Florida Writers' Project, Department of State, Division of Historical Resources, Florida Folklife Archives.

"Raising Popcorn" from Richard Seaman in Gregory Hansen, "The Relevance of 'Authentic Tradition' in Studying an Oldtime Florida Fiddler," *Journal of Southern Folklore* 53.2 (1996): 86.

"Quevedo on French Soil," "Quevedo Chooses to Die of Old Age," "The Tiny Little Chicken," and "The Fig Tree" from Ralph Steele Boggs, "Spanish Folklore from Tampa, Florida: (No. 5) Folktales," *Southern Folklore Quarterly* 2.1 (Mar. 1938): 87–106. Thanks also to Maria Redmon for her translations.

GHOSTS AND THE SUPERNATURAL

"The St. Andrews Bay Legend," "The Witch," "Hugging Molly," "Mystic Music of the Manatees," and "Five-Mile Bank" from Florida Writers' Project, Department of State, Division of Historical Resources, Florida Folklife Archives.

"The Armored Ghost" and "A Christmas Ghost Story" from Sandra Johnson, Leora Sutton, and the Pensacola Historical Society.

"The Woman Who Fed Her Husband a Leg Which She Dug Up from a Cemetery" and "A Ghost Story About an Aunt" from Florida Writer's Project, Library of Congress.

GLOSSARY

Conchs—People born in the Keys, known for their distinctive speech and not their ethnicity, although it originally referred to Anglo-Bahamians. Many of them came from a 1649 group of Cockney Englishmen who went to Bermuda seeking religious and political independence. In the 1700s they migrated to the Bahamas, with many later settling in the Keys. Traditionally, they made their living by fishing and sponging. A main food source was the conch, resulting in the name. Like the conch shell, these individuals are known to have protective shells and rarely move from The Rock (Key West).

Crackers—Self-sufficient individuals, often with Anglo or Celtic heritage, who settled in the rural south, especially Florida. Offspring of these settlers usually carry the name with pride. They are generally known for their independence; they make their living from farming and raising livestock. In Samuel Johnson's 1755 dictionary, the word is defined as "noisy, boasting fellow." In Florida, the name is most often thought to come from the cracking of the whip by cowherders.

Cumulative tale—Story or song where parts are often repeated. These repetitions often link a sequence of events.

Fable—A tale where the main characters are animals that usually take on human characteristics such as speech. There is usually a moral to the story or some kind of worldly wisdom that is imparted. The story is generally short, often satiric and humorous. The origin of fables remains unknown. Fables are popular with children who enjoy learning lessons from birds, bears, rabbits, and other animals.

Fairies—Little people with supernatural power who first appeared in European folklore but were brought to the United States by immigrants. Fairies come in a variety of dress and participate in both festive and solemn occasions. They are often known to grant wishes. It has been said that the only fairy indigenous to the United States is the Tooth Fairy.

Fairy tales—Broadly considered to be folktales like "Sleeping Beauty" and "Cinderella" that may or may not have fairies in them. They include both supernatural and realistic components. There is usually a happy ending where good deeds and character are rewarded.

Federal Writers' Project—Part of the Works Progress Administration that employed writers to document folklore and oral history around the United States from 1935 to 1943. This project was extremely significant to the history of folklore studies in this country. It employed more than 6,500 writers who produced more than 276 books and numerous other publications. Much of our heritage was successfully documented because of this program.

Folklore—An area of study that has been defined in various ways, including "artistic communication in small groups" and "the aesthetics of everyday life." Lists of what the discipline includes have also defined it. Some of the items are myths, legends, folktales, jokes, charms, blessings, riddles, curses, material culture, and rituals. The field of folklore focuses on the documentation and interpretation of various forms of traditional cultural expressions that often go undervalued.

Folklorists—Scholars who study the traditional stories, music, material culture, and beliefs of cultural groups. Folklorists are interested in the creative processes involved in the making, appreciation, and transmission of traditions.

Folk speech—A way of talking that is peculiar to specific folk groups. Folk speech includes grammatical structures, vernacular pronunciations, figures of speech, and localized expressions.

Folktales—A fictional story often used to define loosely all forms of traditional narrative. However, most folklorists use the term to describe more complex narratives. These tales revolve around ordinary people but include fantasy creatures and out-of-the-ordinary circumstances. The best-known folktales are perhaps "Cinderella" and "Beauty and the Beast," which are told around the world in multiple ways. Tellers of folktales often adapt the story to include some of their own personal experiences. In the broad sense of the word, folktales can be known as fairy tales.

Ghost stories—Tales, personal narratives, or legends about creatures that return from the dead. Ghosts may be seen, heard, or sensed, often frightening the unprepared. Many of these stories are linked to specific sites, usually the place where the ghost/person died. In these stories, ghosts come back to this world, either to harm or help the living, to explain the circumstances of their death, or to assist in solving a mystery.

Gladesmen—A group of people who live in the backcountry of the Everglades. Also known as "swamp rats" and "gladeshunters," these independent pioneers are fast disappearing. However, the stories they have told about their experiences in the swampy Everglades live on.

Hurston, Zora Neale (1891–1960)—Writer, folklorist, and anthropologist whose work was inspired by her African American traditions in the South, especially Florida. She also did folklore fieldwork in Harlem, the West Indies, and Haiti. Eatonville, her hometown, now celebrates her life and work with its Zora Neale Hurston Festival of the Arts and Humanities, which takes place each January.

Joot, juke, or juke-joint—Generally refers to an African American gathering place where singing, dancing, game-playing, and storytelling occur, but, in Florida, it can also refer to taverns primarily occupied by Whites. The word "juke" comes from the Gullah-Geechee Blacks of South Georgia and coastal South Carolina and means "disorderly." Often questionable liquor was served, gambling took place, and fights broke out. In the 1930s "joot" was used to refer to any kind of African American gathering that brought people together from neighboring settlements. It could be a simple dance or card or dice game for young people.

Kennedy, Stetson—Head of the unit on folklore, oral history, and social-ethnic studies of the Florida Writers' Project from 1937 to 1942. Born in 1916, Kennedy is also well known as a civil rights activist, an author, and one of the founders of the Florida Folklore Society. His book, *Palmetto County*, is based on his work with the Florida Writers' Project.

Legends—Narratives about the past that usually describe a historical figure or event. Every culture has legends about its own particular heroes and heroines. Legends, therefore, are usually localized. They often deal with the supernatural or characters who possess remarkable powers. Many legends seem believable because of the daily reality depicted in them.

Low bush lightning—Cracker term for moonshine or illegal alcohol. The term probably comes from the copper stills that were hidden in the Florida backwoods.

Myth—A religious narrative that explains the origin of things. The main characters are gods, goddesses, or demigods, and the events that take place in the story help celebrate or deal with the world's existence. While the term has often been used in contemporary times to mean "untrue," a myth, in this context, is not a false belief. For many centuries before that modern definition arose, all cultures valued myths, and they still hold some metaphorical "truth" for particular groups of people in a given time and space.

The Rock—Conch name for Key West.

Snowbirds—People who live in the North and come to Florida to escape the cold. Floridians talk about how they clog the roadways, usually driving very slowly. Natives comment that many snowbirds don't have the good sense to know not to go to the beach in the summertime when it is too hot and the sun is dangerous.

Supernatural—That which cannot be explained by means of modern science. In traditional tales supernatural occurrences may include fairies, witches, ghosts, goblins, curses, magic prophecies, and various kinds of monsters. Supernatural creatures are not always bad. In fact, some, like fairies and elves, are often helpful. Oral traditions are rich in supernatural lore, especially in the southern states.

Superstitions—Folk beliefs, magic, or supernatural lore. It is generally thought to be irrational thinking. All cultural groups have superstitions. Examples include the eating of hog jowls and black-eyed peas by Crackers on New Year's Eve for good luck or an early African American belief that if you cut a child's hair before she is a year old it will affect her speech.

Tall tales—Exaggerated stories that are typically humorous in their absurdity. These tales are often associated with North America's frontier. Tall tales are often told about fishing trips and huge fish that got away. They can be about extraordinarily large fruits and vegetables, strange animals, lucky shots, or remarkable individuals—those with exceptional strengths or the ability to eat or drink a great deal. Extreme weather patterns can also be subject matter for tall tales.

Tellers—Short for storytellers, it usually refers to people who tell traditional tales.

Tricksters—Characters in traditional tales that perform tricks. For the Seminoles the trickster could be the rabbit, and for Florida African Americans he could be Big John or Brer Rabbit. He is clever, undependable, and often untrustworthy. The trickster can sometimes be the target of the trick.

White mule—African American term for moonshine or illegal alcohol.

Wiregrass country—Area of land in the southern United States that begins around Savannah, Georgia, and extends across southwest Georgia and into the northwest part of Florida's Panhandle and the southeastern corner of Alabama. To germinate, wiregrass depends on an ecosystem that necessitates occasional fires. The land and these burning practices are closely tied to a way of life.

Works Progress Administration—Program started by Franklin D. Roosevelt's administration in

1935 that resulted in the largest government-sponsored intervention into the United States' cultural production. It put forty thousand unemployed artists to work in four Federal Arts Projects. These included visual artists, theater workers, musicians, and writers. The Federal Writers' Project resulted in volumes of documented folklore. A few of the stories from this project are included in this book.

BIBLIOGRAPHY

The following sources have been consulted in the preparation of the introductory comments to the tales and the glossary. The list also includes bibliographic materials referenced in the introductions to chapters. Many of these books and articles are recommended for further reading on the topic of traditional tales from Florida.

Akerman, Joe A., Jr. *Florida Cowman: A History of Florida Cattle Raising*. Kissimmee: Florida Cattlemen's Association, 1976.

Allen, Paula Gunn. *The Sacred Hoop: Recovering the Feminine in American Indian Traditions*. Boston: Beacon Press, 1986.

Ammidown, Margot. "Edens, Underworlds, and Shrines: Florida's Small Tourist Attractions." *Journal of Decorative and Propaganda Arts* 23 (1998): 238–60.

Axelrod, Alan, and Harry Oster. *The Penguin Dictionary of American Folklore*. New York: Penguin Putnam, 2000.

Bellah, Robert H., et al. *Habits of the Heart: Individualism and Commitment in American Life*. Berkeley and Los Angeles: University of California Press, 1985.

Bettelheim, Bruno. *The Uses of Enchantment: The Meaning and Importance of Fairy Tales*. New York: Vintage Books, 1977.

Boggs, Ralph Steele. "Spanish Folklore from Tampa, Florida: (No. 5) Folktales." *Southern Folklore Quarterly* 2.1 (1938): 87–106.

Bold, Christine. *The WPA Guides: Mapping America*. Jackson: University Press of Mississippi, 1999.

Brandon, Ruth. *The Spiritualists: The Passion for the Occult in the Nineteenth and Twentieth Centuries*. New York: Alfred A. Knopf, 1983.

Braude, Ann. *Radical Spirits: Spiritualism and Women's Rights in Nineteenth-Century America*. Boston: Beacon Press, 1989.

Brotemarkle, Benjamin D. *Beyond the Theme Parks: Exploring Central Florida*. Gainesville: University Press of Florida, 1999.

Brown, Mary Ellen, and Bruce A. Rosenberg, eds. *Encyclopedia of Folklore and Literature*. Santa Barbara, Calif.: ABC-CLIO, 1998.

Bruce, Annette. *Tellable Cracker Tales*. Sarasota, Fla.: Pineapple Press, 1996.

Brunvand, Jan Harold, ed. *American Folklore: An Encyclopedia*. New York: Garland, 1996.

Bucuvalas, Tina. "The Landscape of Florida Folklife." *Florida Folklife: Traditional Arts in Contemporary Communities, Exhibition Tour*. Ed. Stephen Stuempfle. Miami: Historical Museum of Southern Florida, 1998. 4–11.

Bucuvalas, Tina, Peggy A. Bulger, and Stetson Kennedy. *South Florida Folklife*. Jackson: University Press of Mississippi, 1994.

Burt, Al. *The Tropic of Cracker*. Gainesville: University Press of Florida, 1999.

Coe, Ralph T. *Lost and Found Traditions: Native American Art, 1965–1985*. Seattle: University of Washington Press, 1986.

Daly, Mary. *Gyn/Ecology: The Metaethics of Radical Feminism*. Boston: Beacon Press, 1978.

Dorson, Richard M. *American Folklore*. Chicago: University of Chicago Press, 1959.

Downs, Dorothy. *Art of the Florida Seminole and Miccosukee Indians*. Gainesville: University Press of Florida, 1995.

"Economic Yearbook 2000." *Florida Trends*, Apr. 2000, 56.

Edmondson, Brad. "Immigration Nation." *Preservation* 52.1 (Jan./Feb. 2000): 31–33.

Eliade, Mircea. *Myth and Reality*. New York: Harper and Row, 1963.

Findlay, James A., and Margaret Bing. "Touring Florida Through the Federal Writers' Project." *Journal of Decorative and Propaganda Arts* 23 (1998): 288–305.

Furlong, Lucinda. "Landscape as Cinema: Projecting America." *Visions of America: Landscape as Metaphor in the Late Twentieth Century*. Denver Art Museum and the Columbus Museum of Art, Distributed by Harry Abrams, 1994. 52–69.

Gablik, Suzi. *The Reenchantment of Art*. New York: Thames and Hudson, 1991.

Gallagher, Winifred. *The Power of Place: How Our Surroundings Shape Our Thoughts, Emotions, and Actions*. New York: Poseidon Press, 1993.

Gardner, Howard. *Art, Mind, and Brain: A Cognitive Approach to Creativity*. New York: Basic Books, 1982.

Gates, Henry Louis, Jr. *The Signifying Monkey: A Theory of Afro-American Literary Criticism*. New York: Oxford University Press, 1988.

Goss, James, P. *Pop Culture Florida*. Sarasota, Fla.: Pineapple Press, 2000.

Green, Thomas, A. *Folklore: An Encyclopedia of Beliefs, Customs, Tales, Music, and Art*. Santa Barbara, Calif.: ABC-CLIO, 1997.

Hansen, Gregory. "The Relevance of 'Authentic Tradition' Studying an Oldtime Florida Fiddler." *Southern Folklore* 53.2 (1996): 67–89.

Hemenway, Robert. Introduction. *Mules and Men*. By Zora Neale Hurston. Bloomington: Indiana University Press, 1978. xi–xxviii.

Hurston, Zora Neale. *Mules and Men*. 1935; rpt., Bloomington: Indiana University Press, 1978.

Johnson, Sandra, and Leora Sutton. *Ghosts, Legends, and Folklore of Old Pensacola*. Pensacola, Fla.: Pensacola Historical Society, 1990.

Jones, Michael Owen. *Exploring Folk Art: Twenty Years of Thought on Craft, Work, and Aesthetics*. Ann Arbor: UMI Research Press, 1987.

Joyner, Charles. "Creolization." *Encyclopedia of Southern Culture*. Ed. Charles Reagan Wilson and William Ferris. Chapel Hill: University of North Carolina Press, 1989. 147–49.

Jumper, Betty Mae. *Legends of the Seminoles*. Illustrated by Guy LaBree. Sarasota, Fla.: Pineapple Press, 1994.

Kennedy, Stetson. *Palmetto Country*. 1942; rpt., Tallahassee: Florida A & M University Press, 1989.

Kingston, Maxine Hong. *The Woman Warrior: Memoirs of a Girlhood Among Ghosts*. New York: Vintage, 1975

Kuralt, Charles. *On the Road*. New York: Putnam's Sons, 1985.

Lapham, Dave. *Ghosts of St. Augustine*. Sarasota, Fla.: Pineapple Press, 1997.

Leeming, David Adams, ed. *Storytelling Encyclopedia: Historical, Cultural, and Multiethnic Approaches to Oral Traditions Around the World*. Phoenix: Oryx Press, 1997.

Lévi-Strauss, Claude. *Introduction to a Science of Mythology*. Trans. John and Doreen Weightman. New York: Harper and Row, 1970. (Trans. of *Mythologiques*. Paris: Plon, 1964.)

Linzee, Jill I., et al. *A Reference Guide to Florida Folklore from the Federal WPA Deposited in the Florida Archives*. Collected by the Staff of the Florida Writers' Project and Others with an Introduction by Stetson Kennedy. Compiled by Jill I. Linzee. Edited by Deborah S. Fant and Ormaond H. Loomis. White Springs: Florida Department of State, 1990.

Lippard, Lucy, L. *Mixed Blessings: New Art in a Multicultural America*. New York: Pantheon Books, 1990.

Louis, Liliane Nérette. *When Night Falls, Kric! Krac!: Haitian Folktales*. Ed. Fred J. Hay. Englewood, Colo.: Libraries Unlimited, 1999.

Lowe, Tom. "In Search of Oldest City's Ghosts." *Orlando Sentinel*, Oct. 26, 1997.

Lowenthal, David. *The Past Is a Foreign Country*. Cambridge, Eng.: Cambridge University Press, 1985.

Mander, Jerry. *In the Absence of the Sacred: The Failure of Technology and the Survival of the Indian Nations*. San Francisco: Sierra Club Books, 1991.

Marantz, Kenneth, et al. *The Picturebook: Source and Resource for Art Education*. Reston, Va.: National Art Education Association, 1994.

Matthiessen, Peter. *Killing Mister Watson*. New York: Random House, 1990.

McCarthy, Kevin M. *Alligator Tales*. Sarasota, Fla.: Pineapple Press, 1998.

McDonogh, Gary W., ed. *The Florida Negro: A Federal Writers' Project Legacy*. Jackson: University Press of Mississippi, 1993.

McGregory, Jerrilyn. *Wiregrass Country*. Jackson: University Press of Mississippi, 1997.

McNeil, W. K., ed. *Ghost Stories from the American South*. Little Rock, Ark.: August House, 1985.

Padilla, Marie T. "Florida's Hispanics Outnumber Blacks." *Orlando Sentinel*, Aug. 31, 2000.

Ragan, Kathleen. *Fearless Girls, Wise Women, and Beloved Sisters: Heroines in Folktales from Around the World*. New York: Norton and Company, 1998.

Rawlings, Marjorie Kinnan. *Cross Creek*. New York: Simon and Schuster, 1942.

Reaver, J. Russell, ed. *Florida Folktales*. Gainesville: University Press of Florida, 1987.

Santino, Jack. "Occupational Ghostlore: Social Context and the Expression of Belief." *Journal of American Folklore* 101.400 (1988): 207–18.

Simmons, Glen, and Laura Ogden. *Gladesmen: Gator Hunters, Moonshiners, and Skiffers*. Gainesville: University of Florida Press, 1998.

Siporin, Steve, ed. *Cityfolk*. Salem: Oregon Arts Commission, 1981.

Solnit, Rebecca. "Elements of a New Landscape." *Visions of America: Landscape as Metaphor in the Late Twentieth Century*. Denver Art Museum and the Columbus Museum of Art, Distributed by Harry Abrams, 1994. 100–15.

Ste. Claire, Dana. *Cracker: The Cracker Culture in Florida History*. Daytona Beach, Fla.: Museum of Arts and Sciences, 1998.

Stewart, Susan. "The Epistemology of the Horror Story." *Journal of American Folklore* 95.375 (1982): 33–50.

Storter, Rob. *Crackers in the Glade: Life and Times in the Old Everglades*. Ed. Betty Savidge Briggs and Forward by Peter Matthiessen. Athens: University of Georgia Press, 2000.

Stuempfle, Stephen, ed. *Florida Folklife: Traditional Arts in Contemporary Communities*. Miami: Historical Museum of Southern Florida, 1998.

Tannen, Deborah. *That's Not What I Meant!* New York: William Morrow and Company, 1986.

Taylor, David A. "A Noble and Absurd Undertaking." *Smithsonian* 30.12 (2000): 100–12.

Tinsley, Jim Bob. *Florida Cow Hunter: The Life and Times of Bone Mizell*. Orlando: University of Central Florida Press, 1990.

Toelken, Barre. *The Dynamics of Folklore*. Boston: Houghton Mifflin, 1979.

Toffler, Alvin A. *The Third Wave*. New York: William Morrow, 1980.

Tokarev, S. A. "Toward a Methodology for the Ethnographic Study of Material Culture." *American Material Culture and Folklife*. Ed. Simon J. Bronner. Ann Arbor: UMI Research Press, 1985, 77–96. Translated and Introduced by Peter Voorheis.

Warner, Marina. *From the Beast to the Blonde: On Fairy Tales and Their Tellers*. 1994; rpt., New York: Noonday Press, 1999.

Whisnant, David E. "The Next Phase of Cultural Work in the South: Where We Are, What We Have to Work With, and Where Are We Going." Proceedings from *Promoting Southern Cultural Heritage: A Conference on Impact, December 7–9, 1990*. Ed. Peggy A. Bulger. Atlanta: Southern Arts Federation. 4–11.

White, Deborah Gray. *"Aren't I a Woman?": Female Slaves in the Plantation South*. New York: Norton and Company, 1985.

Wilson, Charles Reagan, and William Ferris, eds. *Encyclopedia of Southern Culture*. Chapel Hill: University of North Carolina Press, 1989.

Works Projects Administration for the State of Florida. Federal Writers' Project. *Florida: Guide to the Southernmost State*. American Guide Series. 1939; rpt., New York: Oxford University Press, 1967.

ABOUT THE AUTHOR/EDITOR AND ILLUSTRATOR

KRISTIN G. CONGDON is professor of art and philosophy at the University of Central Florida in Orlando. She has published many articles and coedited several books: *Art in a Democracy*; *Pluralistic Approaches to Art Criticism*; *Evaluating Art Education Programs in Community Centers: International Perspectives on Problems of Conception and Practice*; *Remembering Others: Making Invisible Histories of Art Education Visible*; and *Histories of Community-Based Art Education*. She has received numerous awards for teaching and scholarship. Kristin Congdon has served as the president of the Florida Folklore Society and was a member of the Florida Folklife Council for eight years. She is currently working on a book on Florida folk artists.

KITTY KITSON PETTERSON always loved reading and drawing and could imagine no finer career than illustrating books. After earning her college degree in writing with the intention of writing and illustrating books for children, life took her in other directions. In 1971, her first painting ever entered in an art exhibition won *Best of Show*. For more than twenty-five years she pursued a career as a painter and graphic artist, exhibiting award-winning paintings in the places where she lived: Pittsburgh, Saudi Arabia, Kuwait, London, and Orlando, Florida. In Orlando she founded and managed a thriving downtown art gallery and events center, where the focus was to provide opportunities for central Florida artists. She also taught college art classes and continued to create and show her own artwork. Though she was sad when she was forced to close the gallery in 1997, she was happy at last to be able to devote her efforts wholly to publishing. She is a longtime member of the Society of Children's Book Writers and Illustrators. This is her first book of illustrations for a major publisher.